David Charlesworth's

FURNITURE-MAKING
TECHNIQUES

David Charlesworth's

FURNITURE-MAKING TECHNIQUES

Guild of Master Craftsman Publications Ltd

This collection first published in 1999
by Guild of Master Craftsman Publications Ltd,
166 High Street, Lewes, East Sussex BN7 1XU

Reprinted 2000, 2003, 2005, 2007

Photography by Robert Seymour unless otherwise credited
Illustrations by Simon Rodway unless otherwise credited
Front and back cover photographs by Chris Skarbon

ISBN-13: 978-1-86108-125-4
ISBN-10: 1-86108-125-1

Printed and bound by Kyodo Printing (Singapore) under the supervision
of MRM Graphics, Winslow, Buckinghamshire, UK

Contents

Note

Every effort has been made to ensure that the information in this book is accurate at the time of writing but inevitably prices, specifications, and availability of tools will change from time to time. Readers are therefore urged to contact manufacturers or suppliers for up-to-date information before ordering tools.

Measurements

Measurements are in metric with imperial equivalents. Readers should be aware that the conversions may have been rounded up or down to the nearest convenient equivalents. Where a measurement is absolute no conversion has been made. *See also detailed conversion charts on page 116.*

Introduction

I was rather surprised and full of trepidation when Paul Richardson asked me to write an article for the first issue of *Furniture & Cabinetmaking* magazine. The prospect of getting to issue 6 seemed remote, but he persevered with his encouragement and inspiration. Without his help I would certainly not be writing an introduction to this collection today.

The aim of these articles is to explore the details of furniture-making and tool use which most textbooks assume knowledge of, or skate over. These are the details which my students struggle with, in their first efforts at fine furniture-making. The advice given here is the result of twenty years of teaching and careful analysis of problems encountered by students. Some of the techniques are innovative and others are arrived at by logical problem-solving and experience.

An area about which I am particularly passionate is plane tuning. Few amateurs can conceive of the improvements in performance, control and finish, which are possible. The work is not particularly difficult, but the results are astounding.

Sharpening and blade preparation are extensively covered. None of my students, however experienced, has ever turned up with really sharp tools. However the techniques described here produce a razor sharp edge without undue difficulty. There is also advice on special techniques for dealing with difficult interlocked timber.

Good quality tools are another obsession. Japanese chisels and replacement plane irons are extensively discussed and I have included details of suppliers. The quality of steel and edgeholding ability of some of these tools is phenomenal and should be of great interest to those who work in difficult timbers.

Several major joints are described in detail and there are three projects which may provide inspiration. I hope you will get much pleasure and assistance from this book, which would not have been possible without the enormous input of editorial work from staff at *F&C*. My thanks to Andrea Hargreaves, Colin Eden-Eadon, Liz McClair and Simon Rodway. Particular thanks go to my friend Bob Seymour for his illuminating photography, also Tim Macaire and Chris Skarbon. Much patience, and primary editing were supplied by Pat.

PHOTOGRAPH BY
TIM MACAIRE

The working

Developing a working shop fit for a cabinetmaker

CABINETMAKING IS an unusual occupation which calls for intense concentration and long hours of solitary labour, so the atmosphere and location of the workshop are of great importance.

As a student, my first experience was of a purpose-built wooden structure in Ted Baly's garden. The view was of tranquil fields, and we had just enough space in which to operate.

My own first workshop was a rented, dry stone barn in the Lake District where the wind whistled through the walls, the light was bad, and swallows presented an unacceptable hazard.

I erected a huge polythene tent within the walls to combat the effects of the wind and the birds – a furnituremaker standing in swallow pooh is not as happy as David Attenborough up to his knees in bat pooh!

Radiant heaters and a Calor gas stove provided heat, but the latter was a disaster as it produced water vapour which condensed on the cold metal of the machinery and tools. Without the draughts, I guess it would have been even worse; the humidity inside must have been very nearly the same as outside – and the Lakes are very damp!

LEFT: The workshop as first encountered...

RIGHT: ...and after a little work.

shop

Moving shop

My twin passions have always been surfing and off-piste skiing, so in 1975 I decided to move to a place where I could work near the sea and surf in my spare time.

All sorts of options were considered; I had hoped to convert a redundant chapel, living upstairs and working downstairs, but there was nothing available near enough to the sea, and planning implications were debatable.

A redundant rural railway station afforded the possibility of a very long pond between the platforms.

I went on visiting as many obscure premises as the estate agents could come up with until, on a still and sunny day, I came across a group of dilapidated buildings, *see photo*, in Hartland and fell in love with the atmosphere of the overgrown and totally enclosed courtyard only 1¹/₂ miles from the sea.

Harton Manor, occupied by the family of the previous owners for 600 years, was in the centre of the village, next door to the pub and the vicarage.

A few paces from the house was a double volume thousand square foot barn which would make a beautiful workshop. In the meantime, a great deal of structural work needed to be done and planning permission

"A furnituremaker standing in swallow pooh is not as happy as David Attenborough up to his knees in bat pooh"

applied for, so it was almost exactly a year before I was able to move in.

Teaching decision

I was completing commissions in oodles of space, and was selected to join the Devon Guild of Craftsmen. However, working on my own was lonely, so when a young man appeared one day, demanding to be taught how to make furniture, I hesitantly agreed to have a go. Nial Gray had found, at that time, there

ABOVE: Bird's eye view of the bench area.

ABOVE: Custom extraction hood for the radial arm saw.

ABOVE: The machine area showing overhead ducting and collector.

"The two dangling handles look remarkably like old-fashioned loo chains hanging above the circular sawbench and bandsaw"

RIGHT: Grinding station and metalworking bench.

FAR RIGHT: Geoff Maiden's bench demonstrates a "level of organisation to which I can only aspire."

were not many workshops taking students.

In an interesting year we started to resolve some of the problems that had been frustrating our technique. We learned a great deal from James Krenov's book *The Fine Art of Cabinetmaking*. Over the years more students appeared, largely by word of mouth, and when my son was born in 1981 I decided to specialise in teaching.

The storage loft was installed, machines moved to their present positions and rudimentary dust extraction installed.

Heating

We used to spend a lot of time carrying logs and tending a Jotul woodburner – one memorable new year's start the temperature was zero; after burning the stove flat out all day the thermometer crawled up to a sweltering 5°C.

Central heating has since transformed the winter environment; thermal underwear and multiple sweaters are now a thing of the past.

Dust extraction

The advent of MDF and the C.O.S.H.H regulations has made good dust extraction a necessity. Our system is not professionally designed but has evolved over the years, and I enjoy trying to improve its performance.

A collection hood for the crosscut saw was specially made, *see photo*. This gathers almost all the dust from this usually messy machine. Because the hood allows the saw to be used only at 90°, work must be supported on wedges for bevel cutting.

The large, red octopus-like duct attached to the ceiling of the machine shop, *see photo*, was built for me by my talented friend Gene Peters.

Dust is directed from the various machines up through this union to a 3hp collector upstairs in the wood store.

The two dangling handles, looking remarkably like old-fashioned loo chains, hanging above the circular sawbench and the bandsaw, cause quite a bit of amusement but are in reality on-off switches connected by a splendidly Heath Robinson arrangement of wires and pulleys to the dust extractor.

The original system was installed by a student over a weekend, and is essentially unchanged.

Vacuum bag press

Gene also showed me how to weld pool liner with the aid of a domestic iron and newspaper. A rudimentary vacuum bag press, which has opened up all sorts of exciting possibilities, was constructed using this technique.

The device is very effective for veneering flat panels, but really comes into its own for laminating curved work – the great

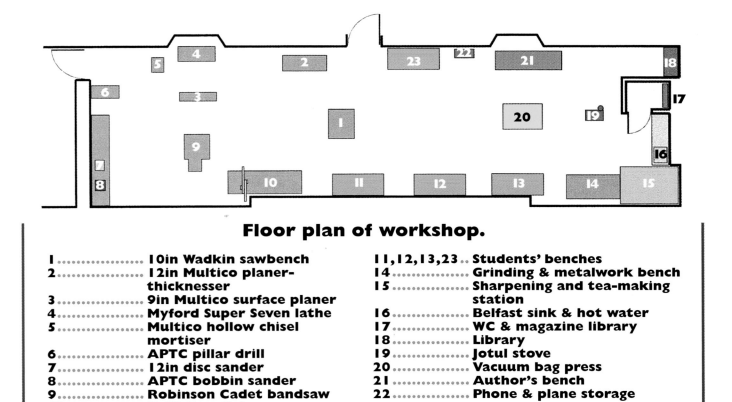

Floor plan of workshop.

1	10in Wadkin sawbench
2	12in Multico planer-thicknesser
3	9in Multico surface planer
4	Myford Super Seven lathe
5	Multico hollow chisel mortiser
6	APTC pillar drill
7	12in disc sander
8	APTC bobbin sander
9	Robinson Cadet bandsaw
10	DeWalt radial arm saw

11,12,13,23 ..	Students' benches
14	Grinding & metalwork bench
15	Sharpening and tea-making station
16	Belfast sink & hot water
17	WC & magazine library
18	Library
19	Jotul stove
20	Vacuum bag press
21	Author's bench
22	Phone & plane storage

"Interestingly, it was the hand skills and tool tuning that fascinated the Scandinavian students"

advantage being that only one half of a former is needed.

Graduates

We have had three delightful graduates from woodworking colleges in Scandinavia recently.

To gain experience in foreign workshops for a couple of months, they obtain travel and maintenance scholarships through their college or government. Two were enrolled at the Karl Malmsten school in Stockholm, where James Krenov studied.

These students were extremely talented and a great asset to the workshop, one building the dust hood for the crosscut saw and two-thirds of a bench as well as a stunning meditation stool (see Seat of contemplation, page 92).

Another built two beautiful pieces of furniture using traditional hand methods. Interestingly, it was the hand skills and tool tuning that fascinated them, and I believe that is what most impressed them about English work.

The immaculate tool board, see photo, belongs to Geoff Maiden, a student who stayed on and operates his business from a room at the end of the workshop.

His bench has been exhibited at the Devon Guild of Craftsmen, where it drew favourable comment from Alan Peters. Geoff's level of organisation, evidenced by his tidy bench, is one to which I can only aspire.

Library

Cabinetmaking is an endlessly fascinating subject about which I am constantly trying to learn more. Several lifetimes would be required to master every aspect so I am always on the lookout for good books on the subject.

We also have a large number of magazines, but because we are running out of shelf space these reside in the loo.

The workshop is constantly evolving and many of the improvements have been suggested by the students. I made a list of them all the other day and in so doing was reminded of all the different characters and personalities who have worked here.

They have enriched my life immensely and it is fortunate that Nial started the ball rolling nearly 20 years ago.

MY FAVOURITE MACHINE

THE ROBINSON Cadet bandsaw was purchased for very little with various parts missing, and has home-made guides – *see photo* – but is quite my favourite machine.

Lignum vitae blocks are used; if touched up frequently these do a superb job. The fence was missing, but for 90% of the time we use a point fence.

A point fence is literally a fence which comes to a point, supporting the work only at the point of cut; this allows the operator to adjust the angle at which the work is fed to compensate for the lead, or cutting direction, of a blade, which can otherwise cause drifting from the cutting line.

Point fences are particularly useful when cutting bandsawn veneer; the ability to do this is invaluable in fine furniture-making as the veneer thus produced will match the rest of the job.

When a straight fence is required, the cutting direction can be checked and a straight wooden fence clamped in position.

Initial vibration was corrected by truing up the vulcanised surfaces of the wheels whilst maintaining the crown which keeps the blade from jumping off.

Please do not try to do this with a blade fitted or under power as either action would be ridiculously dangerous; an assistant is required to turn the wheels by hand.

With a sharp blade and correctly adjusted guides this machine is capable of cutting tenons to within a tenth of a millimetre; we have produced 3mm veneer up to 200mm, eight inches wide and laminates in rosewood (*Dalbergia sp*) of 1.5 mm, $^1/_{16}$ in thick.

The work is pushed down onto the table and, providing one does not feed one's thumbs into the blade, this friendly machine is relatively safe.

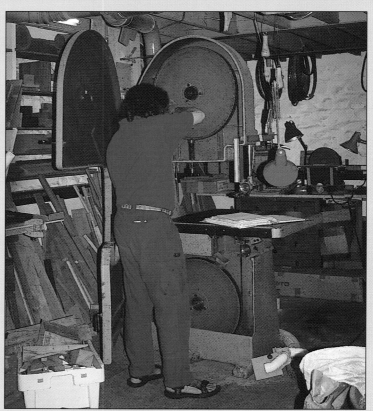

ABOVE: The Robinson Cadet bandsaw.

The latest addition to the bandsaw is the dust collection pipe, *see photo*, positioned right under the throat of the machine and enclosing the blade. A small slot at the back enables removal for blade changing, the whole unit sliding forward when one knob is unscrewed.

This was extremely difficult to arrange but follows the principle of collecting dust as near to its source as possible, and also defeating the problem of the blade and wheels creating wind which sucks the dust round inside the case only to spit it out in your face.

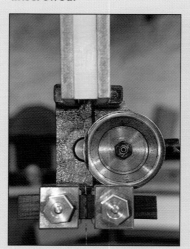

ABOVE: Brass and lignum vitae blocks do service as home-made guides for the bandsaw.

ABOVE: A home-made dust collector is fitted under the throat of the bandsaw.

"…after burning the stove flat out all day the thermometer crawled up to a sweltering 5°C"

Evolution of a

Fine tuning a traditional workbench

THIS BENCH DESIGN has served me well for the past 20 years, and my students have made copies of it for their own workshops as far afield as Sweden, California and Australia.

Finding suitable timber for bench-making is not easy. Beech (*Fagus sp*) is the traditional choice; it is hard, dense and fine textured, but unfortunately rather unstable. A good source of technical data on different species is H.M.S.O.'s *Handbook of Hardwoods*.

If a top is planed flat and true in, say, the spring, it will probably be flat again next spring but will move again in the meantime. Kiln-dried timber helps, and if it is quarter-sawn the stability will be improved.

Central European trees grow tall and straight, so probably the best material is imported.

Using this means that the whole top can be made from four 165mm, 6½in wide lengths which can be up to 2150mm, 7ft long.

Another solution would be to laminate the top out of strips, alternating the heart side.

The bench tops in the photographs have tops made from Doussie *(Afzelia sp)*, a hard, abrasive, difficult-to-work timber, with outstanding stability.

The underframe is made from Iroko *(Milicia sp)*, which is relatively cheap and stable; however, the dust is foul and some people are allergic or can become sensitised to it, so please wear a mask.

Timber thickness

The top can be from 75 or 100mm, 3 or 4in stuff, the legs are from 100mm, 4in and the rails from 75mm, 3in. This may sound like over-building but it makes for a rigid, vibration-free bench.

In the initial machining – a two man job – I like to remove the minimum needed to clean up the timber, so the finished thicknesses are arbitrary.

The height of the bench top should be relative to the height of the user. Mine suits my 6ft 1in height. My suggestion for avoiding backache is about 100mm, 4in below elbow height, standing straight with the forearms horizontal.

Positioning pieces

After the initial machining the position of each piece may be decided for the best visual and structural effect; for a right-handed person this

means that the main slab of the top should have its planing direction from right to left – so that it can be hand-planed clean without too much pain.

End frames

The joinery is straightforward, with the exception of the decorative, recessed, wedged tenons in the front legs, *see illustration*. While these are unnecessary, and could be blind and pegged as in the back legs, they do add interest and act as testimony to the skill of the maker.

I have always found that clients are impressed by a beautiful bench, and it inspires confidence.

Through tenons

The difficulty with through tenons is achieving a good fit on the show side; with these

PHOTOGRAPH BY TIM MACAIRE

bench

PHOTOGRAPH BY
TIM MACAIRE

massive dimensions the friction created is significant. Shaving away the end of the tenon to ease entry spoils the fit at the open end of the mortise.

The solution is to mark out the entry side of the mortise with a layer or two of masking tape added to the gauge, effectively producing a slightly tapered mortise.

Carefully work the tenons, checking their width with dial callipers. If the tenon is a tenth of a millimetre, $^1/_{64}$in smaller than the mortise you won't need a sledge hammer to disassemble the parts, and with joints of this scale the slight taper is a great boon.

Once the cheeks have been fitted the height is cut on the bandsaw, making an easy fit as they will be wedged into place.

The front ends of the short rail tenons are planed and sanded before the slots for the wedges are cut. This surface is set back 4mm, $^5/_{32}$in from the front surface of the legs, with a 3mm, $^1/_8$in chamfer around the mortise opening, *see illustration.* Trimming the protruding wedges flush with the tenon's end after gluing finishes the job.

End frame details

Before gluing up the end frames all the fixing holes may be drilled; the central hole is slotted to allow the main bench top to move.

The sloping fixing hole for the rear bench top is stopped before it emerges from the top of the back tenon, and completed after glue up; this will require a long beam drill.

The seating for the two inch square galvanised washer is perpendicular to the direction of drilling.

The through mortises for the long rail tenons have a sloping top surface for the main wedges. These should be chopped and pared with some

care as they control the stability of the structure.

A special 30° chamfer is used at either end of the sloping surface to prevent the wedges splitting the legs on assembly or disassembly.

Glue up

Use this opportunity to check that all the shoulders close tight and that the whole frame is square and out of wind.

Careful planning and glue-spreading should minimise squeeze out, and the secret of the successful decorative tenon is to remove all the glue before the wedges are driven home.

To clamp the through-tenoned rails four sash cramps are required; special clamping blocks are made to avoid marking the work. The 13mm, $^1/_2$ in holes for the ash pegs which secure the rear tenons are drilled with full clamping pressure applied.

End frame clean up

When everything has been thoroughly checked the final cleaning up, chamfering, sanding, grain-raising and oiling of all

"I have always found that clients are impressed by a beautiful bench and it inspires confidence"

ABOVE: Alternative model with tail vice.

LEFT: Mortises are chamfered at the face for decoration

ABOVE: **Cramping arrangement for wedged tenons.**

I HAVE MOVED the dogs away from the vice on my bench because I got fed up with banging my knuckles on the front jaw when planing. When there is a need to plane long stuff, a simple wooden T square may be fixed in the vice and clamped to the top near the back.

The dog holes may be routed with a simple dado jig if they fall on a join, *see drawing*.

Use of the routing jig does mean that the recess for the pads on the dogs is produced at the same time, with no ledge upon which dust can accumulate.

On the simpler bench these recesses are chopped in after glue up to ensure that the faces are all in a straight line and square to the front edge.

The square, wooden bench dogs, *pictured*, will serve as a planing stop, and are much easier to install if they are on a join; chopping accurate, square holes through the solid is an exacting and arduous task. Round dogs, *also pictured*, need only a drilled hole to sit in, and grip irregular-shapes well.

If using a tail vice two rows of dogs will be useful.

ABOVE: **Square and round bench dogs.**

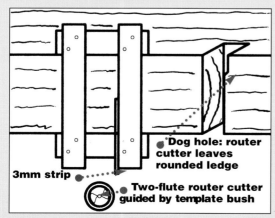

Dog hole: router cutter leaves rounded ledge

3mm strip

Two-flute router cutter guided by template bush

ABOVE: **Simple jig for routing dog holes.**

internal surfaces may be done, the glue surfaces of the joints being cleaned with acetone.

I am tired of reading articles which advocate using chisels to remove excess wet glue. This appalling practice is almost bound to produce blue-black iron stains which have to be bleached out later with Oxalic acid solution.

My suggestion is to sand a 45° bevel on the end of strips of Formica; old toothbrushes are also useful.

The two frames are cleaned up on their three critical surfaces and matched as a pair. First attend to the inward-facing surfaces of the legs where the long rails join, then the front surfaces of the front legs; lastly, plane the top surfaces square to the other two.

The feet – with 30° chamfers to prevent the legs splitting when the bench is dragged along the floor – can be re-marked from the top of the legs.

The top

Carefully machining the parts will save work after glue up. One short dowel in each glue surface provides lengthways location. I am a great believer in hand-planed edge joints, but biscuits or plywood tongues could be employed as well.

With the dowels in place, the main top is held together with a sash cramp for marking out.

Ends, front leg positions, dog positions and the mortise in the underside to hold the vice are all marked with knife and gauge lines; the dogs must clear the front leg by a couple of millimetres, $^1/_{16}$ in.

A shaving off the edges with a sharp plane will give the best surface for gluing, and precise squareness will minimise work later. Ten T bar clamps are placed alternately on top of and underneath the work, which is supported on a pair of large bearers.

A large dead-blow hammer is used to knock the surface of each joint flush.

All the other surfaces are now touched up and checked, the straightness of edges being important. When grooves for the well have been routed, return to the underframe.

Assembly

When the frames and long rails are assembled the wedges are fitted to their individual positions. Sash cramps positioned outside each long rail can be adjusted until the leg frames are square to the rails. Each wedge is tapped into place and then removed.

Examination of the 'polish' on the top surface will reveal any adjustment needed. The whole frame is then inverted and placed onto the underside of the top.

After careful alignment – not forgetting the front and back overhang – it is clamped in place and the coach screws tapped to mark the position for their fixing holes.

The framework may now be pushed clear for the holes to be drilled and the coach screws to be screwed in.

After the vice has been fixed on its packing piece, the jaw extension is glued to the underside of the top, and clamped hard up to the casting which

> "If a top is planed flat and true in, say, the spring, it will probably be flat again next spring…"

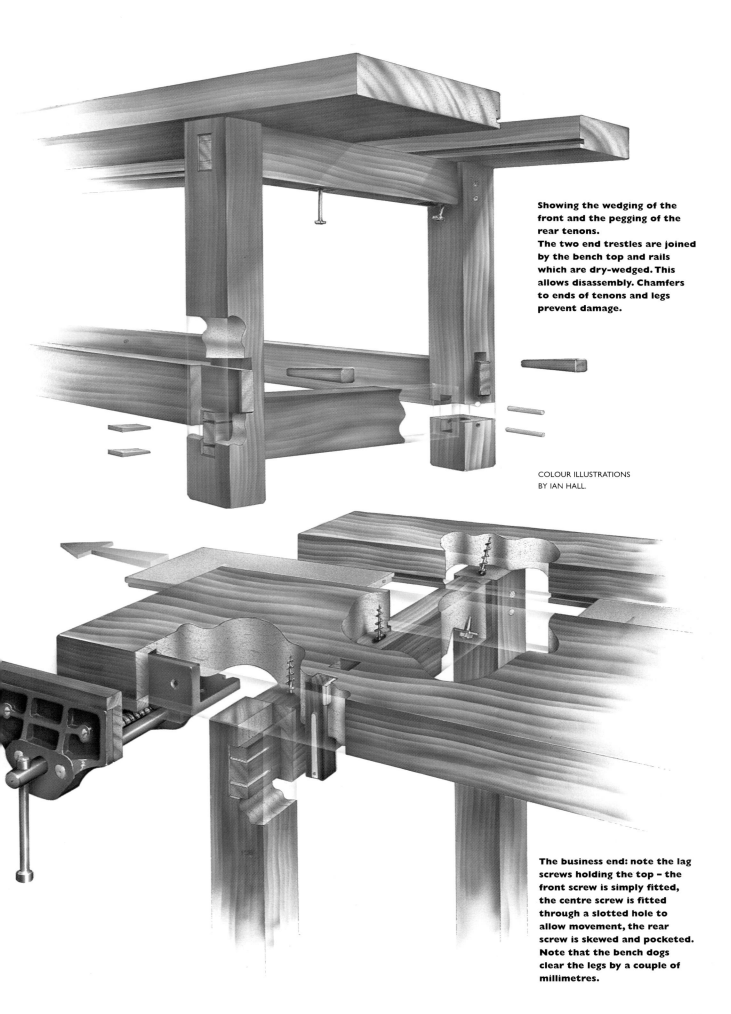

Showing the wedging of the front and the pegging of the rear tenons.
The two end trestles are joined by the bench top and rails which are dry-wedged. This allows disassembly. Chamfers to ends of tenons and legs prevent damage.

COLOUR ILLUSTRATIONS BY IAN HALL.

The business end: note the lag screws holding the top – the front screw is simply fitted, the centre screw is fitted through a slotted hole to allow movement, the rear screw is skewed and pocketed. Note that the bench dogs clear the legs by a couple of millimetres.

ABOVE: Clamping work from the back gives obstruction-free working.

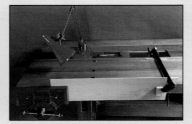

ABOVE: Supporting long stock for edge-planing.

LEFT: Using the bench for veneer-pressing.

> "I have moved the dogs away from the vice because I got fed up with banging my knuckles on the front jaw when planing"

THIS BENCH IS developed from a Rural Industries Bureau design used by Ted Baly and was not without its teething troubles.

I thought it would be useful to have a wider top than the standard 400mm, 16in. This was a big mistake!

The air dried beech (*Fagus sp*) that was chosen came from a local yard and was far from dry. No problem, I thought, I'll laminate the top in 38mm, 1½in strips to combat the known tendency of beech to move around.

The first snag appeared when I started to plane the top as flat as possible and out of wind. I found that it is very difficult to control a plane while leaning at full stretch over a wide bench top.

As time went on another more serious disadvantage became apparent: how to fix the work to the bench. With the conventional arrangement of a fixed tool-well at the back, the only means of fixing is with clamps from the front edge or ends.

Ted had used a Record holdfast which requires large holes to be drilled in the bench top. These give a circular clamping field around each hole, but somehow the pressure from these never seems to be in the right place, and I had visions of my masterpiece developing the appearance of a Gruyere cheese.

I also found these holdfasts tended to displace accurately positioned work when tightened.

The solution

The design brief was clear: a flat, solid and vibration-free surface which had to provide the means of fixing work and jigs over as much of the top as possible, capable of supporting occasional wide work, and including a tool-well.

The solution varied only slightly from traditional design, but to me it's revolutionary.

The main work surface is still 400mm, 16in wide, with a narrow rear support piece 125 to 150mm, 5 to 6in wide.

The key is a sliding, removable tool-well about 250mm, 10in wide, which is divided into four separate panels to make clamping along the back edge of the main top easy.

Usually the outermost panels need only to be slid a short way to provide access for two or three clamps – this has proved particularly useful for jobs like shooting the edge of veneers. In fact a large F clamp will almost reach the centre of the main top so it is

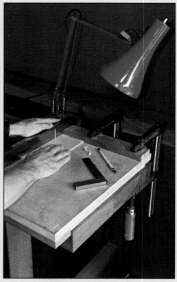

ABOVE: Using bench hook/shooting board to plane end grain of thin stock

possible to clamp over the whole area of the bench.

Keen-eyed readers will notice that the back legs in one of the benches pictured are sloping. This is an earlier version which has now been superceded.

Nothing in this world is unique, and I was fascinated to see a bench design based on a similar idea, on page 97 of *The Workbench Book* by Scott Landis.

is wedged up to the front edge of its mortise.

Final details

All that remains is to stand the bench on its feet, fit and finish the sliding MDF tool-well, plane the top, make the dogs and deal with the front vice jaw, carefully adjusting it until it grips firmly without excessive pressure. ■

Grasping the fettle

The importance of marking-out knives and gauges

NO MATTER WHAT level of woodworking experience my students already possess before coming to my workshop, very few have a proper grasp of marking-out. After timber preparation, this is the next essential step towards successful cabinetmaking, and I teach them that accurate marking-out is likely to lead to a satisfactory result.

"Because the cut surface will be exactly where the knife line was, errors will not creep in"

Knives

One of the main differences between cabinetmaking and joinery or carpentry is that marking-out is almost always accomplished with a knife or a gauge line rather than with a pencil.

Most pencils, unless specially prepared, will draw a line of significant thickness – hardly conducive to precise work – but the beauty of marking out with a knife is that eventually a chisel may be placed in the knife line to make a final paring or chopping cut. Because the cut surface will be exactly where the knife line was, errors will not creep in.

I am often asked which type of marking knife is preferable, a single or double bevel. My answer is that it is ultimately a question of habit and familiarity, the theory being the same for both types.

Like the pencil line, knife lines also have thickness. If a double bevel – Stanley or hobby – knife is held vertical and an attempt made at drawing a line against a straight-edge or set square, the centre of the line will be half the blade thickness away from the straight-edge, *see fig 1*.

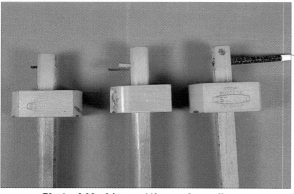

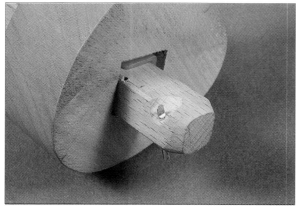

"Marking knives are constantly being worked up against the hard edge of a set square, so frequent sharpening is required and tough steel is a great advantage"

Rules

My first rule of knife theory, therefore, is that the bevel – or surface – of the knife which is against the straight-edge must be vertical – or, better still, leant out by a degree or two, *see fig 2.*

When cutting to this line later it will also be seen that only the vertical face of the knife cut is in the correct place, *see fig 3.* The width of the knife line is obviously exaggerated in the diagram, but it is significant.

Rule two is that the bevel of the knife line should, wherever possible, be towards the waste. Because this rule cannot be observed when marking dovetails, the knife chosen – Stanley or hobby perhaps – should be delicate and the lines not too deep.

For general work, provided these two rules are observed, any type of knife may be used. Lean a double bevel knife outwards, *see fig 2,* but keep a single bevel knife almost vertical, *see fig 4.*

My choice

A variety of knives have proved their worth in my workshop, *see photo 1.* My own is the green-handled blade, which is sharpened with a double bevel and made from very good steel by specialist Sheffield firm George Barnsley, tel 0114 2729263.

It was bought years ago from Parry & Son who have now combined with Tyzack, and is still available from Parry-Tyzack, at 329 Old St, London EC1V 9LQ. Marking knives are constantly being worked up against the hard edge of a set square, so frequent sharpening is required and tough steel is a great advantage.

I have reservations about the standard Sheffield single bevel knife with scraps of rosewood riveted to form the handle. The quality of steel and blade preparation for these knives is poor, they have ill-prepared blades made of poor quality steel, blunt quickly and are hardly suitable for sharpening a pencil.

The third knife shown is a single bevel laminated Japanese knife of particularly hard steel. Great care must be exercised over the angle at which this is held as it is capable of shaving ribbons of steel off the edge of a square! These knives are available left- or right-handed, or a combination of both, in a wide variety of widths.

One of the few outlets to stock left-handed knives is The Craftsman's Choice, tel 01233 501010.

Mike, who is at my workshop at the moment, has come up with a successful method of regrinding a standard knife to convert it to left- and right-hand use, *see photo 2,* and an old HSS hacksaw blade would provide an excellent blank from which to make such a knife.

Technique

When making a knife line the whole hand and wrist should be locked, the drawing being done from the elbow, with the blade surface angled a degree or so from vertical and the heel of the knife a degree or so away from the straight-edge, so that the knife point is up against the straight-edge.

All knives must be sharp and regularly honed. Most have to be sharpened freehand – another exercise in locking the wrists – but my double bevel knife will just fit into a Veritas jig, *see photo 3.*

"When making a knife line the whole hand and wrist should be locked, the drawing being done from the elbow"

Marking gauge

The marking gauge is a simple but much neglected tool. Not user-friendly, they give those new to them considerable trouble, *see photo 4*.

Our modifications take James Krenov's ideas a few steps further. These ideas are also derived from marking knife theory where it is desirable to have the bevel of the knife to the waste wherever possible.

Consider the problem of hand-thicknessing a piece of timber: a standard marking gauge creates a

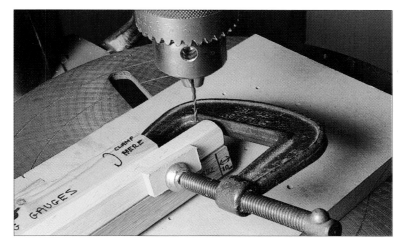

LEFT: Photo 6 Unmodified Stanley 5061

RIGHT: Photo 7 Drilling the new pin hole with the aid of a simple jig

V-groove in the edge of the stuff; planing down to the line, the first notable stage will be a feather edge, *see fig 5*.

Some few shavings later, the V's centre is reached. This centre point cannot, however, be detected too easily, with the danger that the other half of the V could be planed away, leaving

the work significantly under thickness.

Consider instead a gauge where half the pin has been ground away to create a flat side – the remainder of the pin is modified and sharpened to produce a miniature crescent-shaped knife, *see below and Working the Pin panel.*

WORKING THE PIN

The pin is easily removed by fixing the top in an engineer's vice and twisting. The long taper, *see fig 8*, is shortened by grinding a nick and snapping off the excess with a hammer — eye protection essential.

Half the pin is then ground away on the Tormek to create the flat side of the knife, a very slight undercut in the vertical plane being useful, *see fig 8*. We use the simple jig and set-up illustrated, *see photo 9*, which allows the pin to be inspected and returned to the grinder in the same position.

Any grinder would do, but care should be taken to avoid overheating as this would draw the temper of the hardened pin. A spoilt pin may, however, be replaced by a broken HSS drill bit or concrete nail.

The next stage is to grind the remaining half to form the knife. The pin can be held with a small tap wrench, *see photo 10*. Forming a pleasing crescent shape is a delicate operation and it helps if the 'sides' and 'end' are treated separately.

I would suggest that a sharpening angle of about 35° is about right. If the flat side of the pin is lined up with the bar of the tap wrench, the bar will give a useful visual indication of angle while the 'sides' are being ground.

ABOVE: Photo 9 Grinding jig for the flat surface of the pin

ABOVE: Photo 10 Tap wrench used to hold the pin for grinding the bevels

The edges of the 'knife' are polished with a fine slipstone, and the wire edge is removed from the flat side by polishing slightly on a flat slipstone. A permanent black felt tip serves as a useful indicator for many grinding and sharpening

operations. If the ground knife bevels are blacked, it is relatively easy to see when the slipstone is being offered up at a suitable angle. The knife may be tested by dragging it cross-grain over some hardwood scrap. It will cut crisply if sharp and skate if blunt.

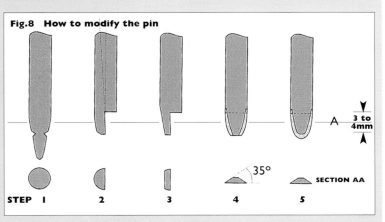

Fig.8 How to modify the pin

STEP 1   2   3   4   5

35°   SECTION AA

A   3 to 4mm

This gauge makes a mark, *see fig 6*. Planing down to the line again reveals first a feather edge and then a step. This step is best viewed by shining a shadow-creating light at a low angle across the surface of the work.

Continue until a polished track can be seen around the edge of the timber. This track, created by the flat side of the pin, will disappear decisively in one final shaving.

Modification snag

The only snag to this modification is that the pin becomes 'handed'. The pin setting for gauging timber thickness is not suitable for marking out rebates or shoulders, as the bevel side would not be towards the waste, *see fig 7,* so the result is twice as many gauges, half with the bevel facing the stock and half with the bevel facing away from the stock.

My own eight marking gauges and six cutting gauges may seem excessive, but I favour relatively cheap gauges, and find it useful to preserve settings during a complicated job.

My latest Mark V modification, *see photo 5,* enables me to rotate the pin through 180° degrees if I run out of a particular type. I recommend that students start with four gauges, two with the bevel in and two out.

> "With the traditional form of marking or cutting gauge, the pin or blade is hidden away under the stem of the gauge"

Wobble cure

With traditional gauges the stock is locked onto the shaft in one plane only, and after some time this arrangement may start to wobble in the other plane. This may be cured by inserting wedges or veneer, but this becomes irritating.

In a damp workshop, the shaft can swell up and become difficult to adjust, but this fault has been designed out of the Stanley 5061 gauge which locks on the diagonal, *see photo 6*.

Grinding and sharpening the pin to form a crescent-shaped knife results in crisply cut lines that will have less tendency to wander and follow wayward grain, *see fig 8*. The tool may now be used across the grain as well as along it.

In effect, a micro cutting gauge which is particularly useful for marking the shoulder lines of dovetail joints has been created.

In show work I prefer not to mark the shoulder line all the way across the outside of the dovetails. With the traditional form of marking or cutting gauge, the pin or blade is hidden away under the stem of the gauge, and it is difficult to start or stop a line neatly.

I used to peer under the stem for the start, and use a rolling thumb as an end stop, frequently removing the gauge to see how far the line had progressed. This long-winded approach explains why the pin on the Mark V has been moved back to exit near the trailing edge, *see fig 11*. The cut-out on the stem also aids visibility.

Stanley 5061

The stems of the Stanley 5061 are usually far from straight, so they should be corrected by judicious planing. A new pin hole may then be drilled, using a simple jig, *see photo 7*.

A drill of about 0.2mm undersize will firmly grip a pin which has been measured carefully with calipers. The cut away for a clearer view is started with a few chisel cuts and finished off with a round file and some abrasive paper.

The final and not so easy task is to adjust the face of the stock so that the face which is pressed tight up against the edge of the work is square to the underside of the stem. An 09 plane is good for this type of work.

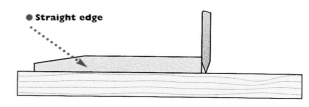

Fig 1 A vertical double bevel knife will give an inaccurate line

● **Straight edge**

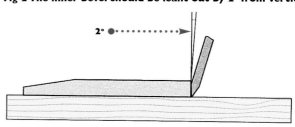

Fig 2 The inner bevel should be leant out by 2° from vertical

2° ●

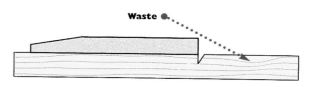

Fig 3 The knife line has width and only the left side is correct. The bevel side should be towards the waste

Waste ●

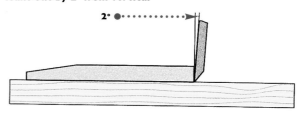

Fig 4 With a single bevel knife the flat side should be leant out by 2° from vertical

2° ●

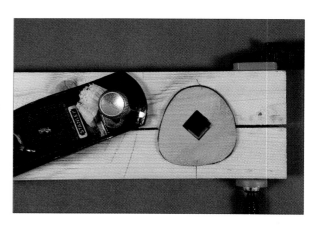

Gauges are much friendlier to use if the pin protrudes a bare millimetre or so. They don't get buried in end-grain or wander off line in coarse, textured timbers. If the stock is not square the pin may be up in the air on a wide setting; the reverse fault is even worse.

ABOVE: Photo 8 Another jig to aid the truing up of the face of the stock

Another simple jig, *see photo 8,* will assist the planing of the face of the stock. Install the pin by holding its blunt end in an engineer's vice while the stem is pushed and wiggled home.

The flat side of the pin may be twisted by about 2° to assist grip of the work, but this only works if the gauge is always pushed in the same direction.

Other gauges

Development of these modifications has produced a much more user-friendly tool. Others are specific to particular tasks, like two interesting Japanese gauges available from The Craftsman's Choice, and an interesting find, a delicate bronze gauge, *see photos 11 & 12.*

FAR LEFT: Photo 13 A delicate bronze gauge found at a market
CENTRE LEFT: Photo 11 Japanese mortice gauge'
ABOVE: Photo 12 Japanese cutting gauge

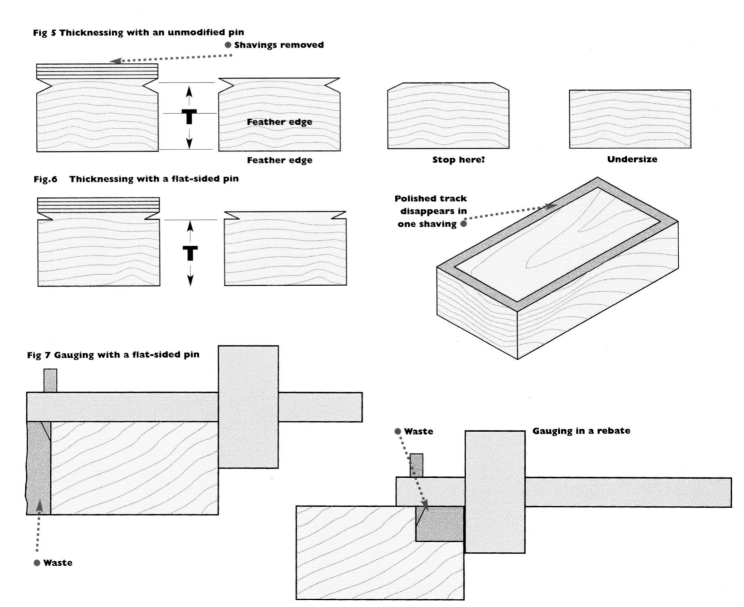

Fig 5 Thicknessing with an unmodified pin

● Shavings removed

T

Feather edge

Feather edge

Stop here?

Undersize

Fig.6 Thicknessing with a flat-sided pin

T

Polished track disappears in one shaving ●

Fig 7 Gauging with a flat-sided pin

● Waste

● Waste

Gauging in a rebate

Spirit of the

The charms of the Japanese chisel

TO ME, Japanese chisels are the thoroughbreds of the hand-tool stable – unless you are lucky enough to own some old, fine, cast-steel chisels of the sort which used to be made in the UK.

The harder the timbers that are worked, the more apparent the difference will be. I have been using them exclusively for the last 15 years, and thoroughly recommend them.

The main difference between western and Japanese chisels is in the blade. European – and American – chisels have a blade which is drop-forged in one piece from a homogeneous steel alloy, while the Japanese version is a laminated structure, forge-welded, or, in some cases, roll-forged at the mill.

This technique used to be employed in the West – I have some old, laminated American Stanley plane irons – but the practice seems to have been discontinued.

The flat of the chisel consists of a layer of relatively pure high carbon steel which is backed up by more malleable wrought-iron or low carbon steel, *see fig 1*.

The support afforded by this backing allows the high carbon layer to be hardened to about Rockwell (C scale) 64, whereas European chisels are hardened to about Rockwell 58 – 57.5. This figure, from Sorby, was the only one I could find.

The junction of the two layers is clearly visible on the bevel of the Nishiki chisel, *see photo 7*.

RIGHT: Photo 1 Long-handled paring chisels, from left, 30mm thin blade by Iyoroi; cranked 18mm parer, dovetail-shaped blade by Iyoroi; 12mm dovetail shape by Koyamaichi; Stanley ⅝in to show scale

"The downside is that they are more brittle and will not stand abuse, such as being used as a lever to prize timber apart"

Samurai

Pros and cons

This extra hardness is highly desirable, as a sharper and longer-lasting edge may be easily produced. The downside is that they are more brittle and will not stand abuse, such as being used as a lever to prise timber apart. If carelessly used, a fairly large chip could break out of the edge, causing much wailing and gnashing of teeth, not to mention a prolonged period of regrinding.

I believe that this explains why British manufacturers have opted to produce a more user-friendly tool, suitable for site work and general abuse by DIY enthusiasts. This is rather sad as Sheffield used to produce superb, top quality cast-steel tools.

The market for hand tools, however, steadily declined, and the 'Little Mesters' have almost entirely disappeared with the exception of a few specialist firms, such as knifemakers George Barnsley, *(see Grasping the fettle, page 14).*

Bristol Design produce some hammer-forged steel chisels, and Clico should also be mentioned for their revival of discontinued tools. The household names that are left, though, seem to be run by accountants who, unfortunately, see no further than the bottom line. Their hand tool lists dwindle every year, and the introduction of mass production has effectively eliminated the small tool maker.

Samurai

This state of affairs has fortunately not yet arrived in Japan, where skilled master blacksmiths are still found in Miki & Sanjo. I imagine that their workshops are not dissimilar from those that would have been found in Sheffield at the turn of the century, although their traditions are unique.

When the Samurai were outlawed around 1870, some of the blacksmiths who forged their swords and spears turned to chisel and plane blade-making. They bought with them a philosophy and spirituality which invested their tools with symbolic importance, as this quote from Toshio Odate's *Japanese Woodworking Tools: Their Spirit and Use* demonstrates: "This heritage is one of the reasons the woodworker's tools are of such high quality and so well known in Japan…"

Chisels are available in a huge variety of qualities, from £10 to over £200 each! The cheapest sets are best avoided, but excellent workmanlike tools may be found in the £20 to £40 range.

As the price increases so does the finish, with the work of art category coming into play at around the £100 mark. These rarefied areas are a bit academic for the majority of us, so I would like to describe some of the chisels which my students and I have been using for the past 15 years.

Long-handled parer

The long-handled paring chisels, *see photos 1 and 2*, are the most approachable; everyone who tries one of these is immediately seduced, their fine balance, thin delicate blades and effortless cutting proving irresistible.

They are only used for paring, and are never struck with a mallet. The extra length allows for sensitive control of the cutting angle and, therefore, of shaving thickness, making accurate paring a great deal easier.

Back preparation

Preparation of the back is a fundamental task for any new edge tool, and some care is required on account of the hollow grinding of the back, *see photo 3*. If the blade is worked across a narrow stone, *see fig 2*, a step will be cut into the narrow areas of the surface.

To avoid this, I like to offer the blade diagonally to the stone so that the top 'island' of metal is also polished, *see fig 3*. The main pressure is applied at the bevel end as we do not really want to remove much metal from this 'island'.

Before starting, check that there is some clearance just above the 'island', so as to prevent the chisel handle riding up on the stone to produce an unfortunate bevel at the tip of the blade.

While most chisels have some clearance incorporated, some do not. If there is none, file or grind a small amount of metal away to create clearance, *see photo 3*.

The 18mm chisel has clearance filed into the shaft. This unorthodox approach solves the problem without significant weakening of the shaft. I discussed this point with tool guru Jim Kingshott recently and we agreed that there is far too little innovation in woodworking circles.

Any solution to a problem is OK if it works for the user. I must emphasise that almost all of my writing is based on pragmatic solutions which have worked here in the workshop; many are unorthodox, but at least I know they work for us.

> "The big firms seem to be run by accountants who, unfortunately, see no further than the bottom line"

Flattening

In my workshop, we start the flattening process on an 800 grit water stone, *see photo 4,* the traditional approach being aluminium oxide grit on a steel flattening plate.

The diagonal position, *see fig 3,* tends to make the back flat, provided the handle is not allowed to ride up on the stone. The stone, however, will soon wear hollow, so let the tip of the blade overhang the edge of the stone for at least half of the time; I allow the tip to travel gently on and off the stone as I work.

As a means of checking whether the width of the blade is flat, I also use the movement pattern shown, *see fig 4.* This technique is particularly useful on a freshly flattened stone, just before changing to a finer grade, say 1200 grit, as it changes the direction of the scratches, making it easier to see if the underlying surface is flat.

The object of the 1200 stone is purely to change the deep 800 grit scratches into finer, more polished, 1200 grit scratches. All the flattening should have been completed before changing stones, so this second stage should take only three to five minutes.

Please be aware that a new chisel is almost never flat, so must be worked for a considerable time on the 800 grit stone – the manufacturer's deep grinding marks must also be erased.

TOP: Photo 4 Flattening the back on an 800 grit stone

ABOVE: Photo 5 Using the Nagura to produce a slurry on an 8000 grit stone

Any coarse sharpening medium would do, but waterstones remove metal faster than any other type, the only snag being that they wear hollow in a short time, so requiring frequent flattening – about every five minutes!

We do this on 240 grit wet and dry taped to a flat piece of float glass. I like to use a variety of movements of the stone as they all have a different effect on the shape of the 'flat' surface of the back.

ABOVE: Photo 3 The 18mm thin paring chisel shows clearance filed into shaft above 'island'. This group also shows how some chisels have multiple hollows ground into the back (san mai), while the 12mm Koyamaichi has a single hollow grind

BELOW: Fig 1 The composition of a Japanese chisel makes all the difference

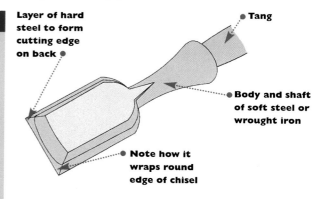

Layer of hard steel to form cutting edge on back

Tang

Body and shaft of soft steel or wrought iron

Note how it wraps round edge of chisel

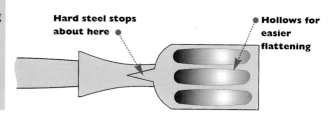

Hard steel stops about here

Hollows for easier flattening

HARDWOOD BEVEL

Because the steel used for the cutting edge of Japanese chisels is so hard, it does also tend to be more brittle. These two properties are inextricably linked, and working hardwoods requires the bevel to be sharpened at about 5° more than for a softer chisel.

I finish my paring chisels at 30° and the chopping chisels at 35°. Heavy mortice chisels may need a 40° or 45° bevel.

The Japanese advocate one single bevel which is worked on the whole range of stones and fully mirror-polished. While this approach will undoubtedly produce the strongest edge, I have not found it necessary for our type of rather delicate work. For the paring chisels we grind at 25° on the Tormek, produce a slight wire edge on the 800 grit stone at 28° and polish the tip of the bevel on the 6000 or 8000 stone at 30°. The flat side is then polished on the fine stone, as for back preparation.

A normal resharpening takes me about four minutes including tidying up and washing my hands! I have read that the steel of these chisels may be damaged if overheated while grinding on an engineer's bench grinder, and although I do not know if this is true, a water-cooled system is much to be preferred. If one is not available I would like to suggest that all 'grinding' could perfectly well be done on a seriously coarse waterstone such as a 220 grit.

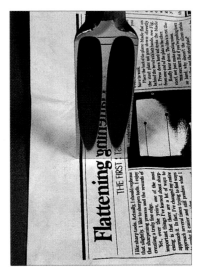

LEFT: Photo 6 Newsprint reflected in the highly polished flat back of a well prepared chisel

RIGHT: Photo 7 A group of striking chisels – the two different layers of steel are clearly visible on the bevel of the unprepared Nishiki chisel at the bottom of the photo; next to it is a dovetail-shaped chisel which is prepared with a seated hoop; students use the 25mm butt chisel and 12mm dovetail chisel by Iyoroi. The 3mm mini chisel is also very useful

If the stones are allowed to dry out a bit at the end of each stage, the slurry will break down into finer particles and produce a slightly higher polish.

Slurry and oil

The final stage is to prepare a muddy slurry on the surface of the fine stone – 6000 or 8000 grit – with the Nagura, *see photo 5*. Because the finer stones should not be kept in water, only sprayed when used, they don't produce the slurry needed; this is created by the Nagura, a chalky paste block; Nagura is not required on stones below 4000 grit.

The movement pattern, *see fig 5*, is necessitated by the sticky slurry on these fine stones. We usually prepare the backs very slightly hollow in their length, so the only parts being mirror-polished at this final stage are the tip and the 'island' at the top of the blade, *see photo 3*.

Clean and dry the blade immediately, and apply a thin coat of protective oil. Non-toxic Camellia oil does a superb job – mineral oils may produce dermatitis in the long term – and marks timber much less than mineral oil if some should inadvertently

stray onto the work.

One of the trade-offs in steel composition is that the extra hardness is gained at the expense of rust resistance. This preparation of the back is somewhat arduous, but well worth the effort as no edge tool will perform to its full potential unless this task has been properly accomplished.

Many of the keen amateurs who come to me on short courses are producing a reasonably sharp edge, but they never seem to be working with properly flattened backs.

The main cause of this condition is a hollow sharpening stone, and the consequent loss of control and performance is disastrous. A well prepared back is shown, *see photo 6*.

Moving hollow

The hollow grinding of the back causes some consternation, as people frequently ask what is to be done when repeated sharpening brings the edge up to the hollow. I wonder how many chisels were abandoned when this stage was reached…

The answer is to return to the coarse stone and work on the back, with the main pressure above the bevel of the chisel.

> "I like to use a variety of movements on the stone as they all have a different effect on the shape of the 'flat' surface of the back"

About 10 minutes' work should 'move' the hollow about 5mm (¹³⁄₆₄in) up the blade.

This operation is not required very often as the steel is so hard that very little needs to be removed at each sharpening. I find that 5mm of blade lasts a very long time as long as excessive amounts of steel are not removed from the bevel during sharpening. For more on sharpening and using waterstones, *see Iron resolve* (page 33).

BELOW LEFT: Fig 2 Clearance and 'island' to allow flattening

BELOW RIGHT: Fig 3 Movement to flatten back

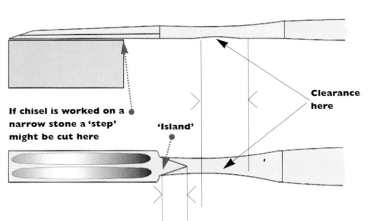

If chisel is worked on a narrow stone a 'step' might be cut here

'Island'

Clearance here

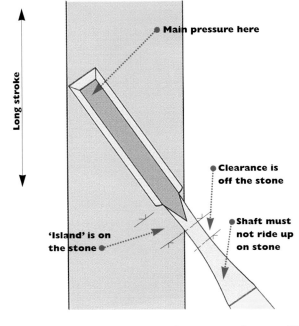

Long stroke

Main pressure here

Clearance is off the stone

'Island' is on the stone

Shaft must not ride up on stone

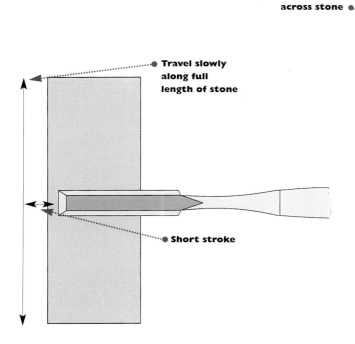

Travel slowly along full length of stone

Short stroke

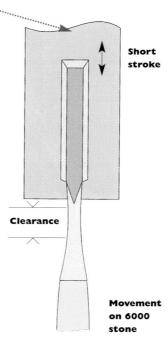

Travel slowly across stone

Short stroke

Clearance

Movement on 6000 stone

"The main cause of an improperly flattened back is a hollow sharpening stone, and the consequent loss of control and performance is disastrous"

ABOVE: Fig 4 Movement to check if chisel is flat across its width

ABOVE RIGHT: Fig 5 Movement to produce mirror polish on chisel back

The handles of the striking chisels used extensively in my workshop, *see photo 7,* are steel-hooped as Japanese craftsmen strike them with metal hammers. I have grown to prefer this method as a hammer has a more concentrated mass, seeming more controllable than even a 4in mallet, *see photo 8.*

Unfortunately these chisels do not come fully prepared, as the craftsman is expected to seat the hoop for him or herself. This process is not, however, entirely straightforward, and the full description is covered in the next article, *Committing Yarri-Kanna,* where I also describe some of the more esoteric chisels available.

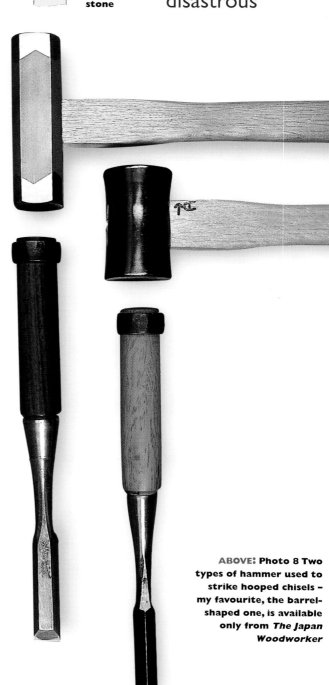

ABOVE: Photo 8 Two types of hammer used to strike hooped chisels – my favourite, the barrel-shaped one, is available only from *The Japan Woodworker*

Committing Yarri-Kanna

PICTURE BY CHRIS SKARBON

Preparing a new striking chisel and other Japanese chisels

I N THIS ARTICLE MY aim is to describe the preparation of a new striking chisel, *see photo 1*, and some of the many other Japanese chisels which are available through specialist suppliers.

The full range – which is too diverse to cover in this article – includes delicate chisels for use when woodblock cutting for printing, carving and sculpting gouges, cabinetmaking tools and larger, stronger examples for boatbuilding and timber frame construction.

Preparation

The preparation of the back of the blade of a striking chisel is exactly the same as for a paring chisel, *see page 19*. A little clearance may have to be filed or ground into the shaft, and the blade may well be shorter unless it is one of the larger temple carpenter's style.

Mike and Dirk, who are here at the moment, have both just bought 36mm chisels of this type and are well pleased with them.

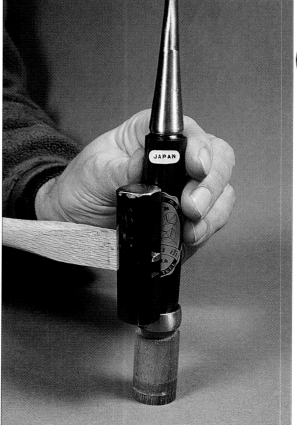

"Try to use one of these tools without seating the hoop properly and it is likely to fall off or create an unpleasant sound when struck with the chisel hammer"

One point I omitted to make in the previous article is that very narrow chisels, say 6mm or under, are probably best prepared with a short stroke, kept in line with the blade. If one tries to move them sideways there is a distinct possibility that the back will start to rock and become rounded in its width.

Nasty finish

One of the oddities of these tools is that the hoop at the top of the handle is not fitted on arrival. Try to use one without seating it properly and it is likely to fall off or create an unpleasant sound when struck with the chisel hammer.

The first thing to do is to tap it off with a small hammer, *see photos 2 and 3*. In this operation, the handle is being supported by a short length of dowel.

SAD AND MUCKY BUSINESS

Oily cloths are potentially liable to spontaneous combustion and should be burned or disposed of safely. I had a sad experience with a customer once. We had decided on a traditional linseed oil finish and he was equipped with materials and printed instructions to continue the process, oil finishing never really being finished.

An old recipe goes: once a day for a week, once a week for a month, once a month for a year and so on.

"The sheen had not been sufficiently glossy for his taste, so in an attempt to hurry things up he had painted on neat linseed oil and left it to dry overnight before attempting to burnish it!"

His table was to have been exhibited some months later, but when collection day came the whole surface was thick with a semi-plastic coating of excess oil.

The sheen had not been sufficiently glossy for his taste, so in an attempt to hurry things up he had painted on neat linseed oil and left it to dry overnight before attempting to burnish it!

The whole job had to be stripped – and a very arduous process it was.

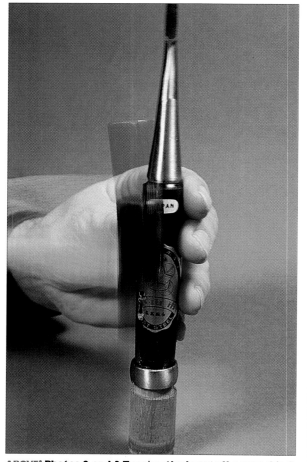

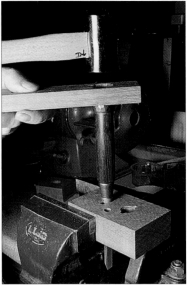

ABOVE: Photo 4 Compressing the handle with a toolmaker's clamp

ABOVE RIGHT: Photo 5 Simple jig used to tap the hoop back on

ABOVE: Photos 6 and 7 Mushrooming the handle so that the hoop stays put

"During these operations the handle may fall off, or a small 'crack' or discontinuity appear in the shaft of the chisel. A recent student was quite sure that he had broken his!"

This is a good moment to remove the horrible finish from the handle, we use wire wool and cellulose thinners. A little careful sanding *with* the grain will remove the turning marks, and some diluted oil will transform the appearance and feel of the tool.

With all oiling operations, the excess must be removed after a few minutes; paper kitchen towel works well. If oil is not removed thoroughly at this stage a sticky, treacly mess will result, *see panel*.

The traditional method of seating a hoop is to compress the timber at the top of the handle by tapping it with a hammer.

This method works fine with the red oak (*Quercus rubra*) handles but is definitely a mistake with ebony (*Diospyrus ebenum*) ones which are easy to split. In fact many Japanese craftsmen would frown on ebony handles as being too brittle. They are properly only fitted to push-style chisels.

The method I have developed is a bit gentler and employs a toolmaker's clamp, *see photo 4*. About 1.5mm (1/16in) of handle should eventually protrude above the hoop so some simple measuring will determine where the hoop should sit.

We wrap several layers of

ABOVE: Photo 8 Structure of a hooped chisel

masking tape to form a small step at this point. Bearing in mind the internal diameter of the hoop, the handle may be compressed by progressively tightening and rotating the clamp.

One or two-tenths of a millimetre oversize will suffice as the hoop needs to be a tight fit. It may then be driven into place with the aid of a simple jig which consists of a piece of hard wood with a hole slightly bigger than the top of the handle, *see photo 5*.

All that remains is to mushroom over the edges of the wood so that the hoop cannot ride up, *see photos 6 and 7*. The textbooks recommend soaking the timber for this operation but I tend to worry about rust and iron stains!

Again, ebony is rather problematical. However, don't be put off it altogether as I suspect these tools will be used rather more delicately by furniture-makers than by a house builder.

During these operations the handle may fall off, or a small 'crack' or discontinuity appear in the shaft of the chisel. A recent student was quite sure that he had broken his!

Anatomy

The main photograph, *see photo 8*, shows the constituent parts of a striking chisel. To remove the handle – not normally necessary – it should be tapped repeatedly against the side of a heavy block of wood.

ABOVE: Photo 9 Standard and double mortice chisels

ABOVE: Photo 10 15mm frame chisel

ABOVE: Photo 11 Square corner-cleaning chisel

RIGHT: Photo 12 Some unusual chisels – harpoon chisel for ejecting chips; bottom-cleaning chisel; sickle for cleaning acute corners

MIDDLE: Photo 13 Bottom-cleaning chisel in use; it is designed to produce a flat base and prevent breakout

FAR RIGHT: Photo 14 A short 9mm paring chisel, a fishtail chisel and a special paring chisel designed by Toshio Odate

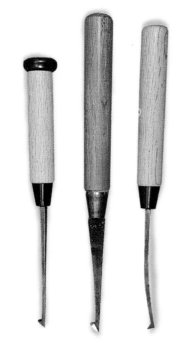

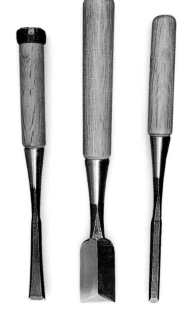

The handle should be parallel to the surface when it strikes the block and the chisel is held by the blade. In fact many handles are slightly barrel-shaped so it is probably the middle which will make contact. A series of firm blows will eventually persuade the friction grip of the wood to release the blade, allowing the tang and tapered ferrule – which stops the wood from splitting – to be examined.

The wood should stop short of the shoulder on the shaft of the chisel by about 1.5mm (⅟₁₆in) so that the tapered section is compressed by the ferrule and grips the tang of the chisel.

This grip transfers the striking force to the blade, *see fig 1*. Also check that the shoulder at the top of the taper is not butted tight to the top edge of the ferrule. Some movement will be required here in very dry weather to accommodate shrinkage of the wood.

Personalised handles

The handle must be able to seat tightly in the tapered sleeve or it will become loose. If there is no clearance a little should be provided by carving back, *see fig 1*.

Please do not be alarmed by these technicalities – we have not found it necessary to make these adjustments over the last 15 years. The first remedy is to plant the chisel in a block of softwood and give it a hearty thump with a hammer! This will usually reconnect things.

I have only recently started experimenting as part of the research for this article, but knowing how to cure a persistently loose handle if the problem arises is useful, and opens up the possibility of making personalised handles.

The square tapered hole which receives the tang is drilled undersize and then worked with a small chisel.

This is not an easy task, and some means of detecting the high spots in the socket, such as soft pencil lead rubbed on the tang, is needed.

Other chisel types

Heavy mortice chisels are virtually unobtainable in this country except from second-hand tool shops and markets, although APTC list one supplier. Some are no thicker than a firmer chisel. The mortice chisel, *see photo 9*, is clearly intended for heavy work. Beside it is a special tool for cutting two evenly spaced mortices at the same time.

I have tried this one out and it is not as difficult to use as one might think! One interesting feature of the mortise chisel is its cross-section, which is different from ours.

The section is rectangular but the sides are hollow ground; this is supposed to give a cleaner finish to

BELOW: Fig 1 Anatomy of a Japanese striking chisel

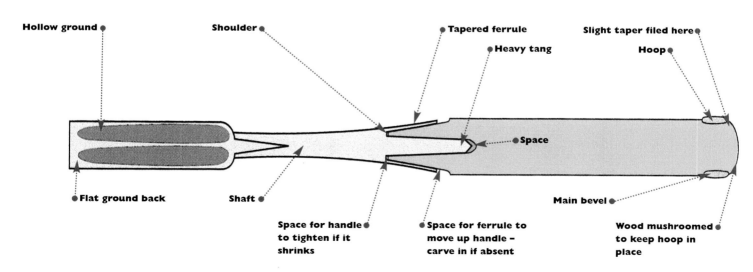

Hollow ground

Shoulder

Tapered ferrule

Heavy tang

Slight taper filed here

Hoop

Space

Flat ground back

Shaft

Space for handle to tighten if it shrinks

Space for ferrule to move up handle – carve in if absent

Main bevel

Wood mushroomed to keep hoop in place

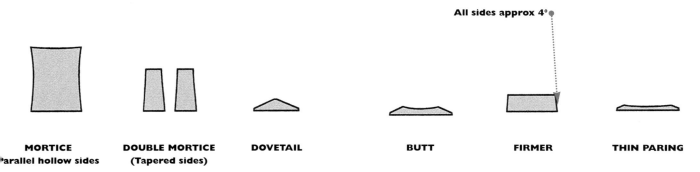

FIG 2 Cross sections of various chisels

All sides approx 4°

| MORTICE | DOUBLE MORTICE | DOVETAIL | BUTT | FIRMER | THIN PARING |
| Parallel hollow sides | (Tapered sides) | | | | |

"I haven't had much luck with my harpoon chisel but it must work well in softwood, which is the material used for Shoji screens and doors"

the walls of the mortice, along with less friction and easier withdrawal from deep mortices.

The double chisel has a section similar to a western tool, *see fig 2*.

The frame chisel, *see photo 10*, is clearly strong enough for morticing.

These are considerably longer than the butt chisels, this 15mm (¹⁹⁄₃₂in) example being 300mm (12in) long with a blade length of 90mm (3½in). Butt chisels are about 225mm (9in) long with a blade length of 60mm (2¼in). Sets are available with dovetail, bevel-edged, firmer and mortice section, *see fig 2*.

A chisel which is used for cleaning up 90° corners, *see photo 11*, is not for heavy work as the bevel is sharpened at a delicate paring angle.

The smaller sizes can be used to square up mortices which have been cut with a router or slot morticer.

Harpoons, sickles

My next group of chisels, *see photo 12*, is most unusual. The harpoon chisel is used to remove waste from a deep mortice rather than levering it out. It is driven into the work at either end, after morticing cuts have been made, then pulled out sharply to eject the waste chips.

I haven't had much luck with this one but it must work well in softwood, which is the material used for Shoji screens and doors. End-grain is considered by the Japanese to be ugly, so mortices are cut almost entirely through the stiles, leaving a bottom which is sometimes thin enough to be translucent.

The bottom-cleaning chisel is used to perfect the base of these blind mortices so that the craftsman does not break through, *see photo 13*.

The sickle chisel is used for cleaning up acute corners. It has applications in dovetail work as well as for cleaning the grooves which hold Japanese plane blades in their wooden bodies. Some other unusual chisels are also shown, *see photo 14*.

Remarkable weapon

I would like to finish with a remarkable-looking weapon which most closely resembles an engineer's three-cornered scraper. I bought one of these years ago when Roger's were the pioneers of Japanese tools in this country.

I sharpened the hollow-ground underside and it sat in my chisel rack for many years, not getting much exercise, but being oiled and discussed regularly as an oddity.

It is apparently the tool that was used to surface timber – after the adze – before planes were introduced to Japan in the mid-15th century. They were used in the sitting position and drawn towards the body with the blade across the direction of movement, a pleasing, undulating, polished surface being the result.

Anyway, one day I was working on some copies of a Barnsley dining chair, and having great difficulty with a small curved detail that was too tight for any of my spokeshaves. In desperation, the spear plane was tried; it proved to be easily controlled and took off precise, delicate shavings, *see photo 15*.

So the Yarri-Kanna finally paid for its keep. ■

ABOVE: Photo 15 Spear plane in use on a flat surface; it is used after the adze in Japan

JAPANESE TOOL SUPPLIERS

To gain an idea of the massive range of tools available, write to Paul Brown at **Thanet Tool Supplies**, Monument Way, Orbital Park, Sevington, Ashford, Kent TN24 OHB (tel: 01233 501010) for a copy of the 86-page *The Craftsman's Choice* catalogue, price £4.95

An interesting catalogue is also available from **The Japan Woodworker**, California, tel 0015 1052 11810, fax 0015 1052 11864.

Two more American companies to try are **Hida Tool & Hardware**, tel 1 510 524 3423, and **Garrett Wade**, tel 800 221 2942 fax 800 566 9525, who also carry a range of Japanese chisels.

Axminster Power Tool Centre, tel 01297 33656 fax 01297 35242, carry two basic ranges of chisels by Iyoroi, and **Tilgear**, tel 01707 873434, stock a basic range by Iyoroi.

Frog and plane body seating

Spending time on your bench plane to achieve ultimate performance

Fine fettle

IN *IRON RESOLVE* (page 33) I hint at Norris-like performance from a standard Bailey pattern bench plane; here I hope to give some hints on how to achieve it. What follows is the accumulation of many years' interest in the subject.

The first clue came when I was working with Ted Baly. A friend had visited a furniture-maker in the Cotswolds, and we were highly amused to hear that this maker sharpened his chipbreaker – but our jesting served only to demonstrate our appalling ignorance.

For some time after my training with Ted, I had difficulty producing perfectly square and straight face sides and edges. I knew exactly what the plane should be doing, but it seemed to have a mind of its own.

The first inkling of enlightenment came from James Krenov's book, *The Fine Art Of Cabinetmaking.*

Over the years more and more snippets of information were gleaned, and I now believe that we make a good job of plane tuning – or fettling.

Lacquer menace

First take off the lever-cap, iron and cap iron, and remove the clear lacquer painted over the surfaces to prevent rust in transit. This lacquer is a menace as it prevents the testing of the sole for flatness; to remove it we use cellulose thinners with wet and dry paper, taking care not to dissolve plastic handles if fitted.

No sole will be flat, but some are worse than others.

The frog may be removed next, noting the torque required to remove the two fixing machine screws; when reassembling later *(see page 30),* take care not to over-tighten these screws, as a distorted sole is the likely result.

The main task here is to check the seating of the frog to the main casting. Once the machined surfaces have been given a thorough clean with wire wool or fine wet and dry paper they should be checked thoroughly for raised lumps caused by dings. A small bevel filed on the sharp corners of the frog seating cures this problem.

Permanent black felt tip may be used – rather like Engineer's Blue – to coat the mating surfaces. If the frog is then offered up into place and ground around a bit, the scraped off ink will indicate exactly where it fits. Adjustment should be made with a fine file and/or engineers' scraper until the contact area is about 75% of the total.

To avoid chatter the centre of the iron must be well supported, so check the top surface of the frog near the bottom of the slope; often this area will be concave. For those not skilled with a file, tape 240 grit wet and dry paper to a flat surface, rubbing the frog onto the paper.

Again, use of felt tip is helpful in judging flatness. A general polish of the whole surface will

> "I am assuming this plane is to be used for the fine finishing of machined boards from medium hardwood all the way up to intransigent interlocked-grain exotics"

LEFT: Close set cap iron

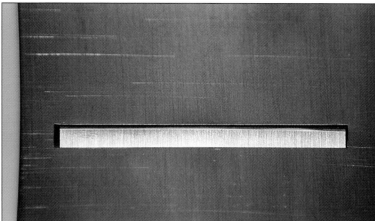

ABOVE: A narrow mouth

ABOVE: Plane
tilted for filing
clearance angle at
front of mouth

"Sod's Law says that something will have moved when it shouldn't so several goes and much patience may be necessary"

also help to make iron adjustment smooth. All sharp corners may be eased with a file, particularly at the top of the slope.

The brass adjustment wheel may also be removed to polish the parts of the Y adjusting lever which contact the brass; 800 grit wet and dry followed by 0000 wire wool and metal polish do a fine job without removing much metal, which would increase the backlash.

Mouth, chipbreaker

I am assuming this plane is to be used for the fine finishing of machined boards from medium hardwood all the way up to intransigent interlocked-grain exotics. In all cases, places where the lie of the fibres is wrong for the selected planing direction will be encountered, and tear-out will ensue.

Where this happens the iron starts a split which runs ahead of the edge and dives down below the surface, *see fig 1*. The finer the setting of the mouth the less tear-out will result, as the sole of the plane immediately in front of the mouth applies pressure to limit the extent of these splits.

The cap iron or chipbreaker acts to break up the splinter, reducing its levering ability – see *Understanding Wood* by Bruce Hoadley for more on this topic.

For fine shavings in difficult timber it should be set very close to the edge of the iron, maybe 0.25mm. If the shaving comes up looking like a concertina, it is too close.

I have never been able to find a theoretical explanation of an optimum angle for the top edge as it meets the iron. However, smoothed and polished modern cap irons seem to end up at about 45° to 50°.

Shaving trap

This causes a potential shaving trap, *see fig 2*, so file the front edge of the mouth forward at 15° vertical to provide some clearance, *see fig 3*. This is done with the plane body tilted in a vice, aiming to keep the file horizontal.

Cast-iron is brittle, so take care when holding the plane in the vice; the jaws should only squeeze the sides gently, where they are supported by the crosspiece web.

On no account should the

opening be made wider than it already is, unless a particularly thick, old iron is to be fitted. We use felt tip again to show where metal is being removed; a lightly scribed line on the sole may also help to keep the edge of the mouth straight.

The corners of the opening may foul the iron if not kept crisp. Extra fine Swiss Vallorbe precision files are perfect for making final adjustments, and are available from Shesto, tel 0181 451 6188.

Polish this surface after filing with the usual sequence of wet and dry paper followed by wire wool and metal polish.

Replacement irons

I discuss replacement irons in *Iron resolve* (page 33).

The thickness of the iron chosen will dictate the ideal width of the mouth – the Hock iron is 2.5mm thick, the Samurai 2.3mm and standard irons are 2.1mm, while an older iron could be much thicker.

I have exploited this fact to give me two different settings on my favorite plane.

The mouth with a Hock iron fitted is about 0.25mm wide, and

"The most important areas are near the mouth where the back of the opening will probably be higher than the front"

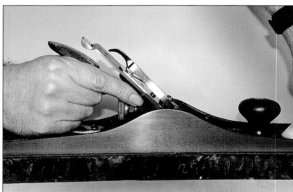

ABOVE:
Flattening and creating clearance on the underside of the cap iron

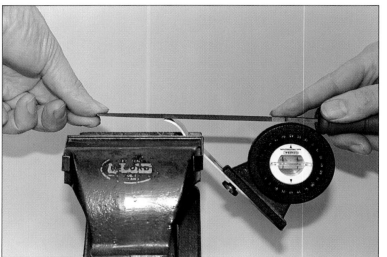

ABOVE: **Filing a smooth curve on the front edge of the cap iron**

ABOVE: **Flattening the sole – using wet and dry paper spray-glued to seriously thick float glass**

with a Samurai iron installed it is about 0.4mm. I select the narrowest mouth for intransigent timbers.

For this reason invest in a replacement iron – Hocks and Samurais appear to hold an edge for twice as long as the standard item – before fixing the frog, as subsequent adjustments to the frog position may upset the flatness of the sole.

Fixing the frog is a delicate and fiddly job, in which the machine screws are replaced and tightened just enough to enable

manual twisting of the frog's position. The chosen cutting iron and cap iron can then be inserted with the lever-cap.

A sharpened iron – ideally possessing a slight curve – is required, as the lateral adjustment lever cannot be used to bring the front edge of the iron parallel to the front edge of the opening.

So the sequence is: set a fine, balanced shaving with the lateral adjuster; advance the frog with its adjusting screw until the mouth is the required width;

twist the whole assembly – without altering the iron settings – to ensure that the mouth is parallel. This done, remove the iron and tighten the frog screws to their final torque *(see page 28)*.

Sod's Law says that something will have moved when it shouldn't, so several goes and much patience may be necessary.

Cap iron

Cap iron preparation is vital for good performance. To ensure a perfect fit with the flat side of the cutting iron (see following article for tips on flattening and polishing this) a slight clearance is helpful – and is easy to achieve if the cap iron is rubbed on a dead flat medium stone while being supported at the appropriate angle.

Again, felt tip may be used as an indicator. As this surface may be slightly twisted, pinch the cap iron to the cutting iron and squint through the gap using a good light source to check for a perfect fit.

The top curved surface may now be worked on with a file to ensure that it meets the underside at an angle of 45° to 50°.

LEFT: **Underside of lever-cap smoothed and flattened**

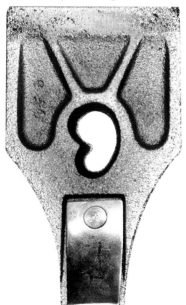

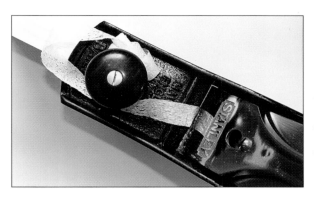

"Being able to remove full-width one thou' shavings from an edge with minimal tear out over difficult grain is rather blissful"

ABOVE: A fine, blissful shaving

When suitably formed, the front 12mm, $\frac{1}{2}$in may be polished to a mirror-finish. All shavings have to glide over this surface so it is worth taking a bit of trouble. Because this part is made of soft mild steel, the two surfaces may have to be worked alternately to avoid a massive wire edge.

Lever-cap

The finish of the lever-cap is often a very rough, plated sand-casting. This surface impedes iron adjustment, but is easily smoothed and flattened on wet and dry paper. It can then be offered up to the cutting iron/cap iron assembly and checked for good contact.

The cap iron surface may easily be adjusted if necessary. If the lever-cap has a lever-operated cam it may also be worth polishing the cam surface and perhaps applying a little wax. Note that some Record planes have a brass knurled screw in place of the lever.

Loctite Nutlock applied to the chrome lever-cap screw, which attaches everything to the frog, cures play. The screw is adjusted so that the lever can be operated without straining the thumb.

If the adjustment mechanism feels too tight, check to see if any of the sliding surfaces could still do with a bit more polishing. Mer car wax provides some protection against rust or acidic hands.

Flattening sole

The most important step, flattening the sole, can be achieved in a number of ways. Gross discrepancies may require initial filing and scraping.

Lapping paste or aluminium oxide powder can be used direct on float glass of at least 6mm, $\frac{1}{4}$in thickness; currently we fix wet and dry paper to float glass with spray adhesive. A truly flat machine table would make an adequate substitute for glass, *see photo 8*.

Start with 60 or 100 grit lubricated with paraffin and work down through 150, 240, 320 and 400 grits to polish after flatness has been achieved. Felt tip lines drawn on the sole will help to reveal bumps and hollows.

Interestingly, Japanese wooden planes are deliberately hollowed in non critical areas, taking account of the fact that only four points need to be in a straight line: the front, the area immediately fore and aft of the mouth opening, and the back.

The most important area is around the mouth, where the back of the opening will probably be higher than the front. Felt tip is removed first from this point. If left proud this back edge of the opening scrapes the surface of the timber; setting for a fine shaving will not produce a cut.

This fault has been rectified when the black lines by the opening disappear at the same rate. Don't worry about hollows between the four points mentioned above, as these will not upset performance. For use with a shooting board, however, working on the sides is worthwhile.

Don't worry too much about squareness – the angle of the work can be adjusted easily – although this could be achieved with the aid of a square support block against which to run the sole of the plane.

I once squared the sides of a plane in this way and found it convenient to set up the whole apparatus on the tilted table of

PLANE SELECTION

FOR THOSE with only one plane I would recommend a 5½ jack, which we have found to be suitable for the majority of our work, although some of our female students have chosen the number 5 for its more manageable weight. While stores

ABOVE: This hand-made Holtey skew-mouthed mitre plane offers perfection straight from the box – at a price

may provide good second-hand tools, beginners can only assess their condition with difficulty, so we usually start with a new Stanley or Record example. I understand that Record have stopped manufacturing the 5½ – a pity as, while more expensive, it was always slightly better finished and seemed lighter. Record are still making numbers 4, 5 and 7. The old Norris, Spiers and Mathieson planes used to cost about the same as a craftsman's weekly wage, so not unsurprisingly today's new plane should be considered only as a kit of parts. But from off-the-peg to couture, Holtey Classic Planes will handmake a superior tool – but expect to pay for the privilege. Contact Karl Holtey at Unit 3, Playingfield Road, Westbury, Northants NN13 5JN tel 01280 709992 email holtey.planes@bigfoot.com

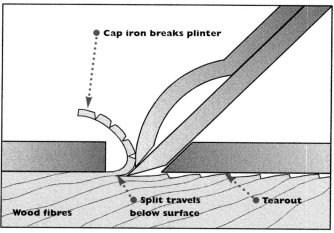

ABOVE: Fig 1 Pressure from front of mouth limits tear-out

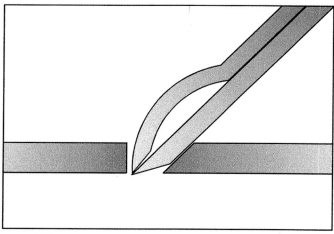

ABOVE: Fig 2 Potential shaving trap when mouth is narrowed and cap iron set close

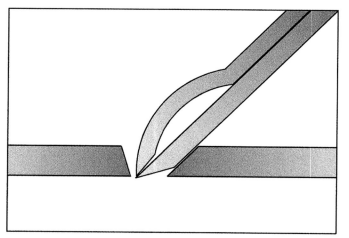

ABOVE: Fig 3 Front edge filed 15° from vertical to allow shavings to escape

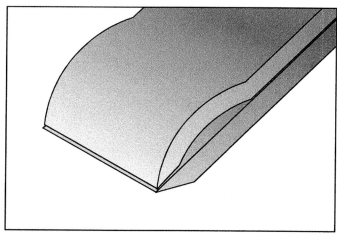

ABOVE: Fig 4 Achieving a perfect fit

the bandsaw. The sole could then be held more easily against the square block.

Sharp edges

The sharp edges of the sole are an invitation for dings, with the inevitable raised bumps which accompany them, and can usually be blamed for repeated scratches running the length of the timber.

Insufficient care in offering up the work to the corners will cause sharp-edged dents. The solution is to file a fair-sized bevel on the front and back edges, and rather less on the long sides.

Similarly, sharp edges at the back of the mouth opening may be eased minutely with fine wet and dry, but don't go too far.

As a final step I like to polish the surfaces with wire wool and metal polish followed with a couple of coats of Mer car wax.

Apply an oil, preferably Camellia, to prevent rusting, brush any debris from the interior, resharpen the iron and take some test shavings.

Being able to remove full-width one thou' shavings from an edge with minimal tear-out over difficult grain is rather blissful. Little effort is required and shimmering shavings swish up through the mouth with a satisfying sound.

Tissue shavings

When I was demonstrating at a show with some sycamore, a young girl commented that the shavings were just like soft tissue paper. Newsprint should be clearly legible through such a

Wave pattern (hollows) on dai sole. Only points 1, 2, 3, & 4 are in a straight line.

ABOVE: Fig 5 Japanese wooden plane

fine shaving – should this performance drop off a bit, check carefully for bumps behind the mouth.

Castings are full of internal stresses from the cooling of the metal, and movement may continue for some years, but with the main bulk of the work done reflattening the sole from time to time should take only a few minutes.

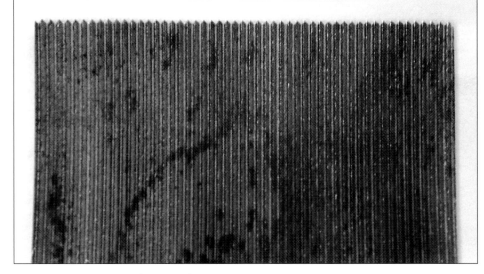

ABOVE: Photo 1 A toothing plane iron illustrates how scratches in the flat side will appear as large nicks in the cutting edge

Iron resolve

An individual approach to sharpening bench plane irons

THERE ARE MANY different opinions and methods published on the subject of plane iron sharpening.

The procedures described below, however, are significantly different, and have been developed in my workshops over the years to enable new students to enjoy the pleasure of using razor-sharp tools.

Several of these techniques are unusual; one in particular was developed here and has never, to my knowledge, been published before. I am referring to the "ruler trick" **which must never be used for chisels**. These require a different approach which is described in *Spirit of the Samurai* (page 18)

The flat side

The cutting edge is found at the junction of two surfaces. The bevel is familiar; metal is constantly removed from it, by means of whatever sharpening system is available.

A highly polished bevel can be honed without difficulty providing that the stone used has a sufficiently fine grit. However, the surface finish on the flat side of a new chisel or plane iron resembles a ploughed field.

Any residual scratches or manufacturer's grinding marks in the flat side will appear at the edge as large nicks — a toothing plane iron illustrates this effect on an exaggerated scale, *see photo 1*.

The 'flat' side is almost never flat as bought, and it is impossible to achieve a polish at the cutting edge until this ideal has been achieved. Effort is wasted on gaining a highly polished bevel if the flat side is not honed to the same degree.

When this is accomplished the edge will appear as a smooth, straight line rather than a jagged edge.

To appreciate this visually some form of magnification is

> "Effort is wasted on gaining a highly polished bevel if the flat side is not honed to the same degree"

required. A pocket 50x microscope, *see photo 2*, is particularly useful for examining the state of tungsten-tipped router cutters and sawblades; however, a child's Lumagny illuminated 30x plastic pocket microscope does the job.

Stone choice

We used to use carborundum oilstones in the workshop, and it was not unusual to spend most of a day on a particularly cussed new iron.

We switched to King brand synthetic waterstones about 10 years ago, and I have also recently invested in the luxury of a large extra coarse DMT diamond stone.

One of the main reasons for the change was to have available a set of stones from coarse to extra fine at an affordable price. I recommend 800, 1200, and 6000 grit plus Nagura, costing £45.47 from APTC, *see photo 3* — also try Tilgear or The Craftsman's Choice, *see panel*.

The very tasty but rather more expensive 8000 grit stone can be substituted for the 6000. A similar range of bench stones of other types — diamond, ceramic

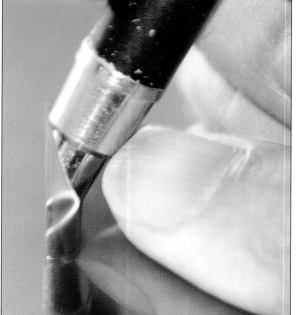

ABOVE: **Photo 2 A pocket 50x microscope used to examine the quality of polish on the flat side, or the quality of the edge**

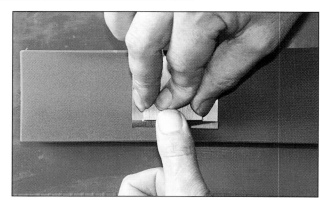

LEFT: **Photo 3 An affordable set of King brand waterstones of 800, 1200 and 6000 grit plus Nagura**

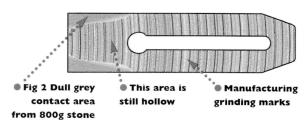

ABOVE: **Photo 4 A wooden handle, fixed with double-sided Sellotape, affords a better grip when flattening the back of a plane iron**

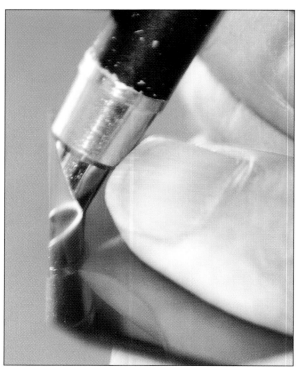

● **Fig 1 Vary the path to evenly wear the stone, turning it round from time to time**

● **Apply pressure here using wood block fixed with double-sided tape**

● **Fig 2 Dull grey contact area from 800g stone** ● **This area is still hollow** ● **Manufacturing grinding marks**

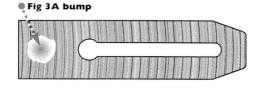

● **Fig 3A bump**

or carborundum plus Arkansas — will cost more but all will produce perfect results.

Waterstones

Waterstones cut much faster than oilstones and will also become hollow quickly; however, they are easily flattened by rubbing — wet or dry — on 240 grit wet and dry paper, taped down to a register surface such as a piece of thick — at least 6mm, $^1/_4$in — float glass.

This flattening should be done as a matter of routine at every sharpening session, rather than being left until large hollows have formed.

The sticky red rubber mat seen in the photographs is a convenient wheeze to stop the stones sliding about on the sharpening area. As waterstone sharpening is a rather messy affair it is best accomplished near a sink, not on the workbench.

These mats are designed to stop plates sliding about on a tray. They work very well if kept reasonably dry.

Flattening irons

Plane irons can be quite difficult to grip without grinding skin away on the stones, so we use

double-sided Sellotape to attach a wooden handle to the bevelled side, *see photo 4*.

A few minutes' clamping provides remarkable bonding. The 800 grit stone must be completely flat for this operation, so check it before starting — it should also be soaked in water for at least five minutes before use.

Applying as much pressure as is comfortable, move the iron up and down the full length of the stone, *see fig 1*. After a few minutes the contact area of the flat side will bear a duller grey scratch pattern.

If the flat side is hollow it will look like fig 2, and if it has a bump it will look like fig 3.

Scratch removal

The object is to spread the dull grey area over the entire edge, removing all of the underlying grinding scratches.

This may take some time so work at a steady pace which can be kept up all day! The stone may be turned round to even out the wear, and should be flattened every 10 minutes or so.

The next stage is to move on to the 1200 gritstone and repeat the procedure with the object of

ABOVE: **Photo 5 Producing a slurry on the surface of an 8000 grit stone with the Nagura**

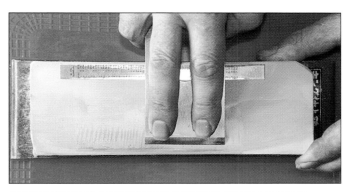

ABOVE: **Photo 6 The ruler trick is used to create a band of mirror polish at the edge**

ABOVE:
Mirror polish

LEFT: **The flattened area**

ABOVE: **Photo 7 The back of a plane iron after flattening and polishing — it should be possible to see the manufacturing scratches, the flattened area and the narrow band of mirror polish produced by the ruler trick**

ABOVE:
Manufacturing scratches

improving the polish. Changing the direction of motion from time to time is helpful, *see fig 4*, as the removal of the underlying 800 grit scratches can be detected more easily.

Ruler trick

Conventionally, the next step would be to polish up the whole flat side on the finest possible — 6000 or 8000 — grit stone, removing all previous scratches.

These fine stones do not need soaking. A spray of water is applied, followed by a paste or slurry worked up on the surface with the Nagura stone, *see photo 5*. This slurry causes a lot of suction between the stone and the large surface area of a plane iron, making polishing difficult.

After some consideration I came up with the idea of cheating a bit and only aiming to polish the leading edge of the flat side, adjacent to the cutting edge. This is done by sticking a 0.5mm, $^1/_{64}$in thick, stainless

steel ruler to one long edge of the stone with the slurry. The iron is then moved laterally, *see fig 5*, with a short stroke across the stone while propped up on the ruler, *see photo 6*.

In this way only the leading edge contacts the stone, and a 2mm, $^5/_{64}$in band of high polish is quickly produced. I know that a very slight angle — maybe 0.25° to 0.5° — has been imposed on the hard-won flat side, but can find no practical disadvantage to this in use.

We now use this method for all plane and scraper irons — but never for chisels, where a pefectly flat back is essential. It is very fast and also constitutes the last step of every subsequent sharpening, *see photo 7*.

Bevelled side

There are many different forms of bench grinders, both wet and dry. The only reason for grinding at all is for speed of metal

> "A sticky rubber mat is a convenient wheeze to stop the stones sliding about on the sharpening area"

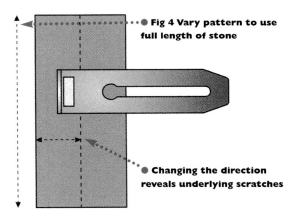

● **Fig 4 Vary pattern to use full length of stone**

● **Changing the direction reveals underlying scratches**

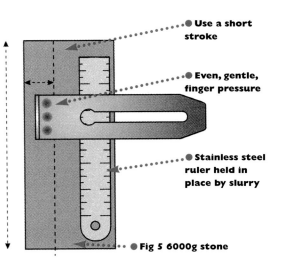

● **Use a short stroke**

● **Even, gentle, finger pressure**

● **Stainless steel ruler held in place by slurry**

● **Fig 5 6000g stone**

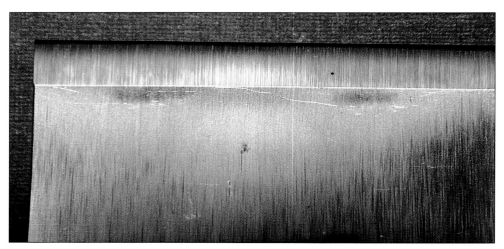

ABOVE: **Photo 8
A 22° grinding
bevel produced on
the Tormek wet
grinder**

ABOVE: **Photo 9 Fingertips applying
pressure near to the edge; they
could be stacked. By varying this
pressure point and the number of
strokes used, a curved edge may be
produced**

removal; the same result could be achieved on a very coarse stone.

I can thoroughly recommend the larger Tormek wetstone machine which has banished the dreaded bluing — from overheating — from our edge tools.

With all grinders it is important to have some means of dressing and truing the surface; a glazed wheel cuts slowly, generating excess heat which is even more likely to draw the temper of

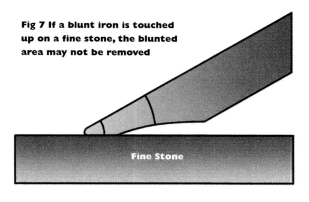

● Fig 6 **The wire edge is a tiny
burr formed when the
old edge has been
honed away**

800g stone

Fig 7 **If a blunt iron is touched
up on a fine stone, the blunted
area may not be removed**

Fine Stone

hardened steel.

Most engineers' bench grinders are greatly improved by changing the wheel for a coarser, softer, cooler type. Ours is a pink wheel of 60 grit.

We grind the bevel at a lower than normal 22°, taking care to stop the grinding just before the cutting edge is reached so as to prolong the iron's life, *see photo 8.*

Honing guides

Unlike some, I am a firm advocate of honing guides, particularly for beginners. Because the honing angles can be precisely set and repeated, only the minimum amount of material is removed at each resharpening; this saves time and effort as well as steel.

If regrinding is not required, a normal sharpening takes me four minutes, including washing and tidying up.

I do not believe that the free-rolling wheel of a honing guide hollows the stone; this results from tool pressure — besides, flattening the stone is a vital routine anyway.

I particularly recommend the Eclipse honing guide as its narrow wheel allows the user to control the pressure at the tip of the iron and thus the shape of the edge, for example when honing a

"Most engineers' bench grinders are greatly improved by changing the wheel for a coarser, softer, cooler cutter"

square edge on a narrow chisel. Wider wheels, such as those of the Veritas model, dictate the angle and cannot easily be tilted, although this may be an advantage in some cases.

When using any guide, pressure should be applied with the fingertips near to the edge and not over the wheel, *see photo 9.* The dextrous may employ their thumbs to relieve pressure from the wheel.

Wire edge

To achieve a wire edge on the 800 grit stone, set the plane iron in the guide at an angle of 30° — the relevant projection, 38mm, is printed on the side of the Eclipse — and draw the iron towards the body, using as much of the length of the stone as possible.

This motion is repeated until a slight wire edge is formed. This may be visible by directional light, or it can be felt by sliding a finger tip over — not along! — the edge of the flat side.

A satisfactory edge feels like a small hook as if the iron has been burnished like a scraper, signalling that enough metal has been removed to get past any previous wear or rounding of the edge, *see fig 6.*

If an iron is merely touched up

ABOVE: **Photo 10 The sharpening bevel formed and polished**

> "After some consideration I came up with the idea of cheating a bit and only aiming to polish the front edge of the flat side adjacent to the cutting edge"

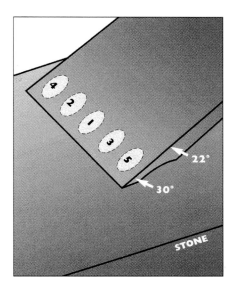

RIGHT **Fig 8**
The circled numbers indicate the different positions used to apply pressure with the forefingers to form a curved edge

on a fine stone this may not be the case, *see fig 7*. A wire edge may be achieved in three or four strokes when a freshly ground iron is employed. At each subsequent sharpening it will take more strokes, as the width of this bevel increases, until eventually a regrind will be needed, starting the cycle again.

Curved edge
I am a strong advocate of the slightly curved plane iron, *see photo 9*, and use of the 800 gritstone enables the curve to be formed.

Let us suppose that the wire edge has been produced — step 1 — see above. The forefingers applying pressure near the edge are now stacked on top of each other and used to apply point pressure, *see fig 8*.

Metal is removed principally where pressure is applied. Try six strokes with pressure just inside the outer edge in position 4, repeat in position 5 — step 2 — then apply three strokes with pressure in position 2, repeating in position 3 — step 3.

The slight curve produced may be examined by offering the edge up to a flat surface. We use a bit of aluminium extrusion; the light showing under the outer edges should be about 0.25mm, $^{13}/_{64}$ in, although varying degrees of curve may be used for different types of work. If the curve is not big enough repeat steps 2 and 3.

When resharpening a curved iron, start with the pressure in position 1 and count the number of strokes required to produce a wire edge. The same number of strokes should then be used in positions 2,3,4 and 5.

Quick polish
Polishing the cutting edge on the finest stone may be done extremely quickly if the angle of the iron is increased to 35° — Eclipse guide projection 32mm. I have found no disadvantage in using this slightly steeper angle, indeed I find it extremely helpful for hard and abrasive timbers.

The iron is now curved, of course, and the 6000 gritstone is flat, so three strokes are used with gentle pressure at all five positions. No more than this is required as only the tip of the previously achieved 30° bevel is polished.

Finish with the ruler trick on the flat side, dry and oil the iron and enjoy the razor sharp edge, *see photo 10*. ▪

Useful Contacts
● *The Craftsman's Choice,*
tel 01233 501010
fax 01233 501201
● APTC, tel 01297 33656,
fax 01297 35242
● Tilgear, tel 01707 873434
● The Japan Woodworker,
U.S.A. tel 0015 1052 11810,
fax 0015 1052 11864
● Bristol Design,
tel 0117 929 1740
● Karl Holtey,
tel 01280 709992

REPLACEMENT IRONS

THE NON-STANDARD iron in photo 7 is of a high carbon steel, hardened to Rockwell 62, made in California by a knife-maker called Ron Hock.

The need for a better quality iron becomes apparent when planing the end-grain of timbers such as ebony or lignum vitae; with a standard iron the edge folds up and is shredded almost after the first shaving, unlike the better quality replacement which offers twice as much service.

We also use Japanese 'Samurai' laminated irons which are slightly thinner, but the extra thickness of Hock irons is particularly beneficial in low angle block planes and spokeshaves as it helps to minimise chatter.

My source for Hock irons is The Japan Woodworker in California, *see left*, whose catalogue is an Aladdin's cave. Another alternative would be old cast-steel irons from a specialist such as Bristol Design, *see left*.

When I visited the school at Parnham House, Robert Ingham told me about an Australian Stanley high speed steel iron, which had performed well. Unfortunately I have not yet been able to track one down. There are now three thicker blades available; Lie-Nielsen, Victor and Holtey. The Holtey blade outperforms the rest in abrasive timbers.

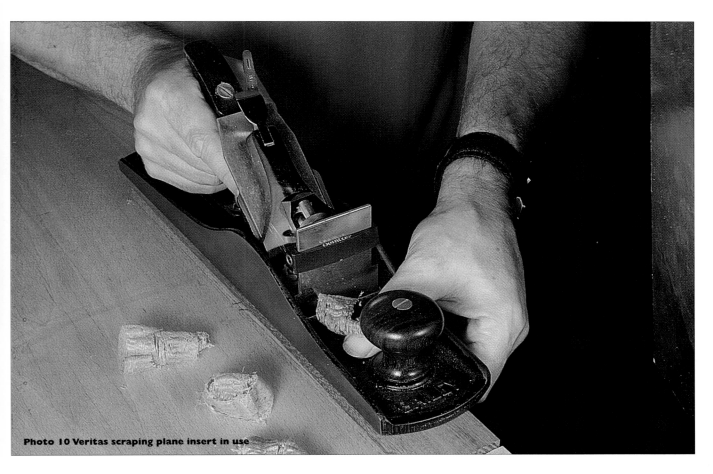

Photo 10 Veritas scraping plane insert in use

Scraping in

Ways of dealing with difficult grain

USING A HAND plane to remove fine shavings from well-mannered stuff is therapeutic and rewarding. Sadly, however, many of the more glamorous and visually interesting timbers consist of grain structures which do not respond well to hand-planing.

When tearout occurs calm satisfaction is replaced by mounting frustration, so this month I am offering various strategies for dealing with the problem, using standard kit.

When students first encounter the terrors of tearout I always say, "When the going gets tough, machine and scrape" – and that means starting with the planer.

The main culprits seem to be some of those timber suppliers who offer a machining service. One student, for instance, arrives with planed-up timber from his supplier which is bowed, out of square and, worst of all, torn out to a depth of about 1.5mm (¹⁄₁₆in).

> "When tearout occurs calm satisfaction is replaced by mounting frustration"

Arduous planing corrects these faults, but the secret is to minimise hand work by taking fine cuts with a carefully prepared machine planer. The preparation can then be perfected with a couple of sets of shavings by hand.

Sharp practice

I hate changing planer knives, finding the process of alignment tedious. Sharpening, however, takes no more than 20 minutes and rewards with a better finish and less hand-planing.

The following technique does require a machine with an adjustable out-feed table. With each sharpening the effective cutting radius of the knives is reduced slightly, so the out-feed table must be re-set accordingly.

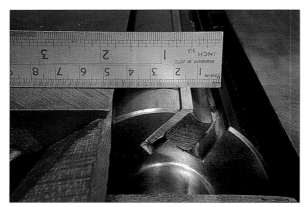

ABOVE: **Photo 1 Knife lifts ruler by 0.5 mm – note wedged cutter block**

ABOVE: **Photo 2 Oilstone in position for honing knife, cloth protects machine table**

ABOVE: **Photo 3 Slipstoning a micro bevel on flat side of blade**

ABOVE: **Photo 4 15° bevel on flat side of plane iron being honed with Eclipse guide**

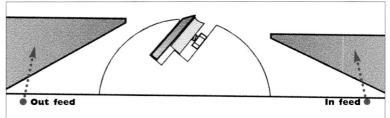

● **Out feed**   **In feed** ●

"Beware of honing at any steeper angle, as clearance will be lost and the heel of the bevel will pound and glaze the timber instead of the edge cutting it"

Isolate machine

The first step is to isolate the machine, remove its fence and guard, then lower the out-feed table to the level of the top of the cutter block, *see fig 1*. A steel rule is helpful, *see photo 1*.

After winding down the in-table, turn the cutter block anti-clockwise until one knife lifts the steel rule about 0.5mm clear of the cutter block. The cutter block is then gently held in this position with a hardwood wedge, *see fig 2*.

Now measure the distance from the edge of the knife to the edge of the out-feed table, noting it so that the other blade(s) may be wedged in the same position later. Record the measurement on the 'carry forward stick' for later use.

RESETTING THE PLANER

The knives of a surface planer must move a steel rule or accurately planed wooden stick forwards by about 3mm when the cutter block is rotated by hand.

Surely, some have said, the knives should be dead level with the out-feed table? Not so. The confusion on this matter is caused by failing to consider the feed rate of the timber and the lack of more than two or three knives. The planed surface of the timber is thus not flat but composed of a series of scoops. The high points rather than the low points must rest flat on the out-feed table, so the top dead centre of knives must be slightly above the level of the out-feed table.

Experience suggests that the ideal amount of carry forward varies slightly for different timbers, hard dense exotics requiring slightly less than soft springy ones.

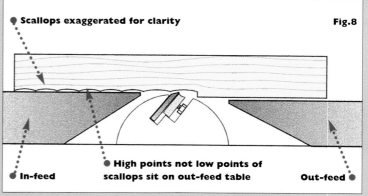

● **Scallops exaggerated for clarity**   **Fig.8**

● **High points not low points of scallops sit on out-feed table**

● **In-feed**   **Out-feed** ●

ABOVE: **Rotary cutters at work – top dead centre of knives is not level with finished surface**

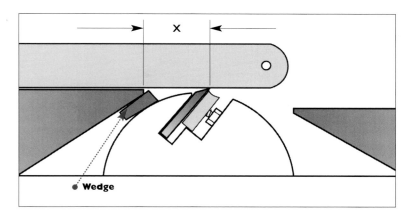

LEFT: Fig I Set-up for planer sharpening to modified angles. In-feed table lowered 15mm, out-feed table lowered to height of cutter block

RIGHT: Fig 2 A steel rule is essential for accurate setting up of the cutter block
Step 1: Cutter block is rotated anti-clockwise until knife lifts rule 0.5mm
Step 2: Wedge cutter block in position
Step 3: Measure and note distance X to match with other knives on block

As the blades are repeatedly sharpened, this figure is gradually reduced so as not to hone a wide surface. A fine 20 by 50mm (8 by 2in) oilstone, with some rag wrapped round the end to protect the out-feed table, is used to hone HSS knives, *see fig 3 and photo 2*. For tungsten blades a diamond stone may be substituted.

Marking the bevel with black felt-tip pen provides a useful indicator for checking that the edge is being honed. If it is not, the cutter block will have to be rotated a bit more. Our knives are ground at 35°, the honing being close to 40°.

Beware of honing at any steeper angle, as clearance will be lost and the heel of the bevel will contact and glaze the timber instead of the edge cutting it.

> "The micro bevel does not need to be wide to be effective, but because a reduced cutting angle requires more power, the feed rate may have to be cut"

To hone, make perhaps six rotations of the oilstone in an oval pattern, each set of ovals being centred on and between the bolts securing the blade, *see fig 4* .

Wire edge

Aim to produce a small wire edge on the flat side of the knife, taking careful note of the number of passes required so that the same amount of honing can be done on the other knives. Next hone the flat side with a small, fine India slipstone, *see photo 3*. A word of caution – a slip will result in a very nasty cut. I like to use short strokes and work gradually across the length of the knife.

Wrap Sellotape around the slipstone to avoid honing the cutter block. The slipstone is supported on the cutter block and on the slightly worn securing wedge, *see fig 5*, so achieving a repeatable angle. The honing pushes the wire edge back onto the bevel side of the blade where it may be rather more easily felt by a fingertip brushed across the bevel. If no wire edge can be felt, the bevel honing should be repeated.

This wire edge may also interfere with table setting so lay it down with one more pass of the bench stone; a single set of rotations should knock off the wire edge when the machine is used. The cutting edge should now be much sharper.

The whole procedure is now repeated exactly on the other knives, and both machine tables are reset to their original positions, *see panel*.

Micro bevel

This process produces a micro bevel, which effectively reduces the cutting angle of the knife – resulting in a scraping action ideal for machining difficult interlocked-grain hardwoods.

This machine technique has its parallel in hand-planing, when the pitch angle of a bench plane or moulding plane is increased, *see my article on the Holtey York pitch smoothing plane on page 54.*

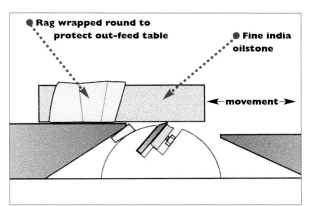

ABOVE: Fig 3 Honing position of oilstone

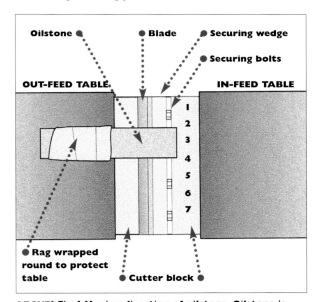

ABOVE: Fig 4 Honing direction of oilstone. Oilstone is moved in oval pattern, six rotations in each of seven positions gives even honing

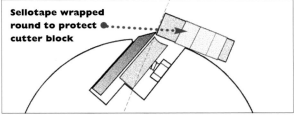

ABOVE: Fig 5 Position of small oilstone for honing modified angle on flat side of knife

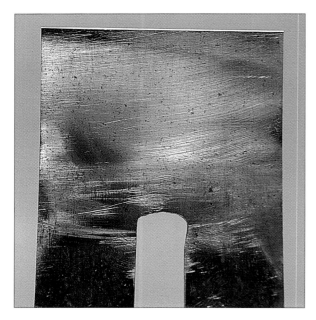

ABOVE: **Photo 6**
Old cast-steel iron
with flat side
bevel of 30°
clearly visible

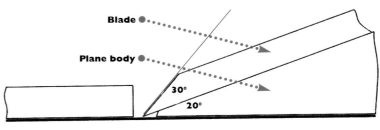

E.P = 20° + 30° = 50°

ABOVE: **Fig 6 Effective pitch of 50° for a 9½ block plane**

"Properly sharpened hand scrapers are wonderful tools, but in the hands of the unskilled are invitations to disaster"

The micro bevel does not need to be wide to be effective, but because a reduced cutting angle requires more power, the feed rate may have to be reduced. This technique may be unsatisfactory for use with some softwoods, although it copes with cedar of Lebanon (*Cedrus libani*).

Effective pitch

That the effective pitch angle of a block plane may be modified by sharpening the blade at an increased angle is a well-known fact. As the effective pitch angle is increased, more of a scraping action is induced, causing less tearout.

It is worth considering the effective pitch angle of block planes rather carefully. The 60½ 'low angle' block planes have an effective pitch angle of (12.5 + 30), 42.5° if sharpened at 30° – only 2.5° lower than a bench plane.

The number 9½ block planes have an effective pitch angle of (20 + 30) 50°, *see fig 6*, which can easily be increased to 60° by sharpening the iron at 40° – great for timbers such as ripple or 'fiddleback' maple.

Many years ago I increased the effective pitch angle of a bench plane by honing a small bevel on the flat side of the blade.

To do this place it upside down in a honing guide; a flat, narrow bevel is created on either a coarse or medium stone and then polished at the same setting on a super-fine stone, *see photos 4,5 & 6.*

Because I have not exhaustively tested all the possibilities, and each timber species will have its own character, I am being a bit vague about the precise angle required, *see figs 7a and 7b.*

The lowest bevel angle convenient in an Eclipse honing guide is 15°, giving an effective

ABOVE: **Photo 7 Stanley No. 80 scraper**

BELOW: **Photo 5 10° bevel on flat side with General (off-stone) guide**

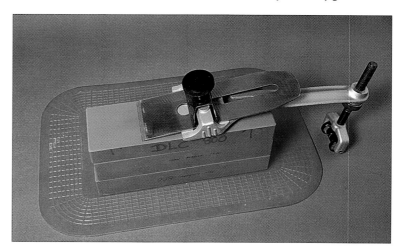

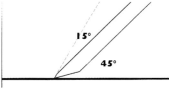

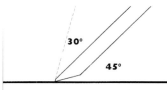

E.P = 15° + 45° = 60°   E.P = 30° + 45° = 75°

ABOVE LEFT: **Fig 7a Effective pitch of 60° for bench plane, good for most woods**

ABOVE RIGHT: **Fig 7b Effective pitch of 75° – an extreme scraping angle for woods like lignum vitae**

pitch of 60°. I have used a bevel of as much as 30°, producing an effective pitch of 75°, for planing impossibly interlocked lignum vitae (*Guaiacum officinale*); all I can suggest is experimentation.

"Beware of an alarming snapping noise as the flexed blade escapes at the end of each shaving!"

Steep effective pitch angles do, however, make the plane harder to push and require a fine setting to avoid chatter. The benefits of being able to produce untorn surfaces on woods like rosewood (*Dalbergia* sp) and ebony (*Diospyrus ebenum*), however, far outweigh these minor snags. Note that this technique will not work well on softer woods.

Hand scrapers
Properly sharpened hand scrapers are wonderful tools, but in the hands of the unskilled are invitations to disaster, particularly so if a synthetic finish which needs rubbing down between coats is used on the finished piece. In this case the high spots will be rubbed through to the timber and the low spots will not be touched.

My preferred option is to use the Stanley No. 80 scraper plane, *see photo 7*, and to take sets of shavings off the whole surface until the problems are solved, *see photo 8*; this maintains flatness and also avoids burnt thumbs.

For best performance the blade should be sharpened to the same degree of polish as a bench plane blade. It is also necessary to flatten the tool's sole.

Blade-setting can be a little awkward; the main difficulties in use are starting and finishing the shaving. Slight skewing of the tool and careful transfer of weight will help to prevent it tipping up and catching the end of the work in the excessively wide mouth.

Because the sole is a little short it may be worth making a wooden scraping plane, for which excellent plans are given on page 91 of Bob Wearing's *Making Woodwork Aids and Devices,* (revised edition published by GMC Publications, ISBN 1 86108 129 4).

Plane insert
The recently introduced Veritas Scraper Plane Insert, *see photos 9 and 10*, provides another option. This device drops into a bench plane in place of the blade and chipbreaker and works in a similar manner to the Stanley No. 80, thus solving the short sole problem.

Blades for this are available in two thicknesses and to suit two widths of plane, 2in or 2⅜in. They are sharpened at 45° before a hook is burnished. The flat side preparation of these scraper blades is a bit difficult as they are thin at 0.4mm and 0.6mm.

I achieved an even distribution of pressure when polishing the flat side by fixing a small, rectangular, MDF handle to the opposite side with double-sided Sellotape. The clear instructions must be followed carefully when the sharpened blade is fixed into the device.

The apparatus is then loaded into the plane where it is controlled by the normal blade adjusters. A fine adjuster, which I suspect may be redundant, is built into the device. I prefer the thicker blade although both work well, producing tissue-thin shavings, but beware of an alarming snapping noise as the flexed blade escapes at the end of each shaving! ■

ABOVE: **Photo 8 Stanley scraper plane in use**

BELOW: **Photo 9 Veritas scraping plane insert**

"Wind is pronounced with a long 'i' and has nothing to do with flatulence"

How to unwind

Producing a reliable face and edge

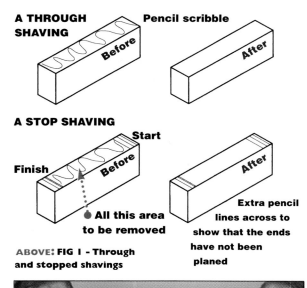

A THROUGH SHAVING

Pencil scribble

Before

After

A STOP SHAVING

Start

Finish

Before

After

All this area to be removed

Extra pencil lines across to show that the ends have not been planed

ABOVE: FIG I - Through and stopped shavings

ABOVE: Using a straight edge and a slip of paper to measure the degree of hollow in the length.

ALL FURNITURE construction relies on the accuracy of the planed timber. This provides the reference points for cutting, jointing and fitting, so if a mistake is made early on it will be magnified as a cumulative error until the fit of a door or drawer becomes little more than guesswork.

Nowadays we are used to the 'almost right' produced by a machine planer – but with a well-prepared bench plane this can be improved to the point of 'bang on' quite quickly. When the timber has been machined to within a few millimetres of finished size, a face side and face edge must be assigned to each piece. These will be the reference points.

First a face side is created – this must not only be straight but also flat – in three stages: length, width and diagonal.

Length

With a No. 5 or 5½ jack plane, take a couple of through shavings (one end to the other) to remove machining marks.

Next, try deliberately to hollow the

length by removing sets of stop shavings – starting and stopping within the length – until the plane stops cutting. Perfect flatness is a theoretical concept not much found in the real world, so a slight hollow should be aimed for. This stops the set square from rocking and thus producing more than one reading. Test the amount of hollow with a slip of paper under the centre of a straight edge – *see picture*. This will measure approximately one-tenth of a millimetre, which is about right.

Having done this, take a series of through shavings to remove the stop-shaving marks, then re-test with the straight edge.

Width

If the stuff is relatively narrow, say up to twice the width of the plane, a similar policy of deliberately trying to hollow the width can be used. A set of shavings is removed from the whole surface except from the edges.

Start in the centre and work outwards, using a pencil scribble across the wood to ensure that the edges are not removed.

METHOD 1 – TESTING FOR FLATNESS

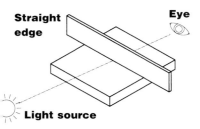

Straight edge

Eye

Light source

METHOD 2

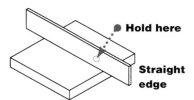

Hold here

Straight edge

ABOVE: FIGURE 2 – Using the straight edge – relative merits of sighting and pivoting

TOP VIEW

Gently slide from side to

RIGHT: FIGURE 3 – Straight edge pivots on bump

High point (bump) – static or pivot

TOP: Winding sticks in use.

ABOVE: Considerable wind revealed.

BELOW: A full width shaving from an edge.

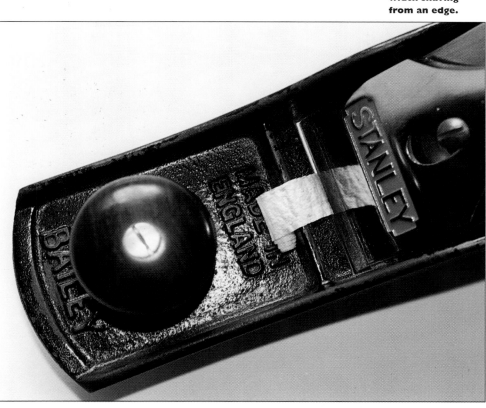

A wider board will necessitate identifying and marking high spots with a straight edge – which will spin or rock on these bumps – *see fig 2*. This is a better indicator than looking for light under the straight edge, and involves less bending. Mark high spots with pencil and plane them away mainly with through shavings.

When finally satisfied, a set of through shavings with a sharp, fine-set blade will even up the surface.

Diagonal

The last remaining problem with our surface is that it may be twisted or 'in wind'. This is pronounced with a long 'i' and has nothing to do with flatulence.

The easiest way to detect this fault is by use of winding sticks. These are made by the craftsman and are essentially two straight sticks of stable timber with parallel edges. Mine have inlays of white acrylic in the top edge of the far stick, and a background of dark matt wood fitted into a groove in the top edge – *see picture.*

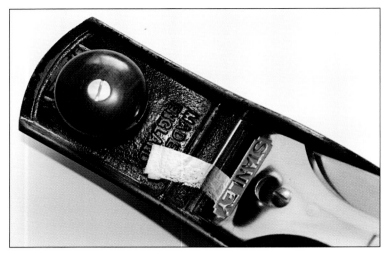

"If any reader can explain to
me how a square edge is
produced with a straight blade
– other than with a shooting
board – I would be most
grateful..."

The sticks are placed across the
job at either end and the observer
sights along their tops.

If there is no wind the tops of the
sticks will be seen to be parallel.
Where wind is apparent shim up the
low corner of the far stick with
scraps of paper until the error
disappears; this gives a
measurement of the amount of
timber to be planed away to
correct the error.

Let us suppose that two scraps
of paper corrected the wind. This
is equivalent to four standard
shavings – these must be removed
without upsetting the straightness of
length and width already achieved.

If the high and low corners are
marked it is obvious that the high
corners must be removed and the
low corners left alone, but to avoid
introducing bumps into length or
width shavings must be taken all the
way up to the low points. If the stuff
is not too large the whole surface
except the two low corners can be

CURVED EDGE

A RELATIVELY fine setting should be made, which will produce shavings of one twentieth of a millimetre. To do this, check the thickness of the shavings with a pair of dial calipers. This Rabone Chesterman glass-filled plastic model is affordable and will, if used with care, give excellent results.

In my workshop a tenth of a millimetre is considered a heavy shaving, half a tenth a standard shaving and a quarter of a tenth is set for fine finishing of difficult grain.

A tenth of a millimetre is about four thousandths of an inch – which happens to be the thickness of a normal sheet of paper. This is convenient as a slip of paper can be used as a feeler gauge. A tenth of a millimetre seems a reasonable tolerance for fine work.

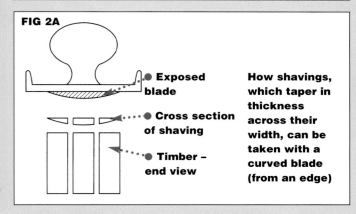

FIG 1A

The slight convex curve of the plane blade

Straight edge

0.25mm   0.25mm

The amount of curve can be varied for different types of work

FIG 2A

● **Exposed blade**

● **Cross section of shaving**

● **Timber – end view**

How shavings, which taper in thickness across their width, can be taken with a curved blade (from an edge)

My preference is for either a No. 5 or No. 5½ jack plane, with the blade sharpened to a slight convex curve. If the work is long there is an advantage in using a longer plane, such as a No. 7, as it is less likely to follow undulations in the surface.

This allows a tapered shaving to be taken off at either side, and an even shaving at the centre.

---

planed – very long stuff will require a different approach.

In our theoretical example the shaving pattern would be repeated twice in order to remove a total of four standard shavings, so correcting the two sheets of paper error that was detected.

The surface is tested again with the winding sticks and, if satisfactory, another set of through shavings is taken to clean up the stop-shaving marks.

After re-testing straightness of length and width, remembering that a slight hollow is preferable, a face mark is applied before proceeding to the face edge.

Face edge

The length of the chosen edge is hollowed and through shavings taken as for the face side.

It is now necessary to test for squareness from the face side. Grip the set square firmly and press the centre of the stock firmly against the face side.

With the work held up to a good light source, slide the stock gently downwards until the blade touches some part of the edge. The blade should be perpendicular to the length of the edge.

Test each end and at four inch intervals inbetween. Mark the high points with pencil.

Place a narrow shim of paper under one edge of the blade to see what an error of a tenth of a millimetre looks like.

Here comes the cunning part: exploit the slight convex curve of the plane blade to remove the errors of squareness from the edge of the piece of timber by moving the plane on and off centre as the edge is planed – *see "Curved edge" panel.*

If any reader can explain to

me how a square edge is produced with a straight blade – other than with a shooting board – I would be most grateful...

If the edge is high on the right, then it is planed with the centre of the blade slightly off the right-hand side of the edge. The shaving appearing in the mouth can be

BELOW: A full width shaving from end grain using a No. 60½ plane – the thumb-centred grip is mandatory here

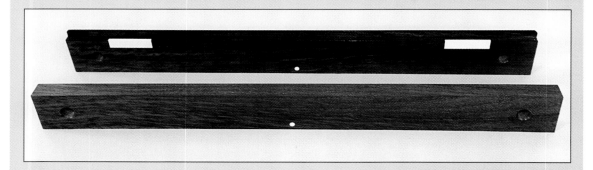

FIG 1B – MY WINDING STICKS

**Sonokoling rosewood –
white acrylic inlay –
background of African
ebony**

● cl ● cl

● Hanging holes – 8mm countersunk

Background ebony,
no glue, push fit ●

8
33

4mm dia. ●

8

2

1.5

● White acrylic inlay   ● cl

23   14

34   35

● Inlay 1.5mm thick

380

THESE WINDING sticks are made from rosewood (*Dalbergia sp*) with a white acrylic inlay and a background strip of African Ebony (*Diospyros sp*).

The background strip is not glued in place and is left loose in its groove so that it may be removed, allowing the top edge of the winding stick to be planed true from time to time.

The dot inlay at the centre of each stick helps to centre them on narrow stock.

> "If the edge is still square at the end award yourself many gold stars"

seen to taper to zero thickness over the left-hand side of the edge – *see picture*.

When high on the left the procedure is reversed; deal with a twisted edge by starting to one side, drifting onto the centre where the edge is square, and then drifting off to the other side.

Get a grip

A variation of the usual grip on the front end of the plane is helpful for this job. Thumb pressure must be centred over the middle of the work's

edge to keep the sole of the plane flat to it – *see picture*. I never use the front knob for edge planing.

When satisfied with the squareness along the edge, take a central through shaving, watching both edges of the shaving to see that a full width of cut is maintained. Re-test for straightness and apply a face edge mark.

To test edge planing technique, start with a square edge and take 10 through shavings. If the edge is still square at the end award yourself many gold stars. On wider stuff –

wider than the amount of blade that is exposed – sets of shavings will have to be taken, as in the face side procedure.

Straight and true

You should now have a truly straight, square and flat face and edge which you can trust. It will provide the necessary foundation for immaculately fitting joints.

I find hand planing with a well fettled plane and a sharp blade to be a therapeutic and satisfying pastime – a chance to unwind as I unwind. ■

Plane and simple

How to get the best out of your low-angle block plane

I CAME ACROSS the following passage in a web site on the history of Stanley planes. It refers to Stanley's marketing propaganda which claims:

A Block Plane was first made to meet the demand for a plane which could be easily held in one hand while planing across the grain, particularly the ends of boards, etc. This latter work, many carpenters call blocking-in, hence the name Block Plane.

This, if it is to be believed, dispels the myth that block planes are so named because they were first used on butcher's blocks.

Block planes
Block Planes are an interesting and useful group of tools, *see photo 1*, in which the blades are mounted with the bevel side up. This arrangement allows the blade to be supported much closer to the cutting edge, by the machined surface, which is an integral part of the sole – it having no removable frog, *see fig 1*. This support minimizes chatter, or blade flexing, and does away with the need for a chipbreaker. The low-angle planes, of 12.5° bed, are ideal for planing end-grain, while those bedded at 20° are good for difficult surface grain. If the blade is honed at 27°, the low-angle plane has an effective pitch of 39.5°, whilst the 20° bed, with a blade honed at 30° has an effective pitch of 50°.

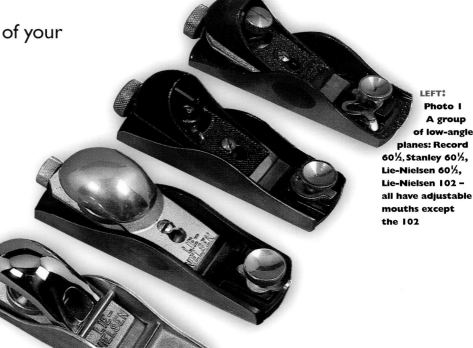

LEFT:
Photo 1
A group of low-angle planes: Record 60½, Stanley 60½, Lie-Nielsen 60½, Lie-Nielsen 102 – all have adjustable mouths except the 102

Replacement Irons
I never used to have much joy with my Stanley 60½ block plane on hard end-grain, but tended to use a bench plane instead, except for short wide sections which couldn't be shot with the aid of a bench hook. A major breakthrough occurred when a Hock replacement iron was fitted which reduced the tendency to chatter considerably, and the operation became more controllable and satisfying. The improved edge-holding ability was beneficial, and the extra thickness of blade helped too. Hock blades are 2.4mm whereas standard blades are 2.1mm thick. At this point I was finally converted to the advantages of the low-angle plane. I am engaged in an ongoing discussion with Paul Richardson about these matters and we are both convinced that blade thickness has

a huge impact on plane performance. This has recently been reinforced by my testing of the Lie-Nielsen No 62, low-angle jack plane, *see photo 13*, and tests done with Karl Holtey's special, thick blades (2.8mm) for bench planes. Fortunately Lie-Nielsen planes do not need replacement irons as they come equipped with high quality, thick, surface-ground irons hardened to Rockwell 60-62.

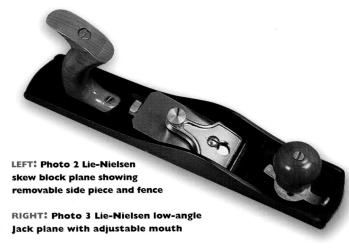

LEFT: Photo 2 Lie-Nielsen skew block plane showing removable side piece and fence

RIGHT: Photo 3 Lie-Nielsen low-angle Jack plane with adjustable mouth

RIGHT: **Photo 4 Checking the seating of the adjustable front sole with engineer's blue**

FAR RIGHT: **Photo 5 Centre punch marks to tighten a sloppy fit**

BELOW: **Photo 6 Checking blade seating with engineer's blue – and a good view of a home made eccentric mouth adjuster**

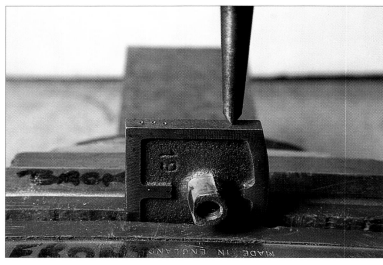

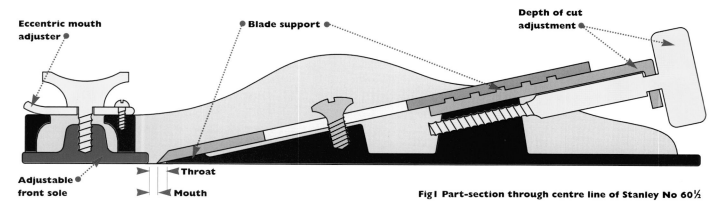

ABOVE: **Photo 7 Blade seating being corrected with a fine file. Note how the angle of filing is assisted by a wooden support block wedged into the adjustment support**

Adjustable mouth

An adjustable mouth is a valuable feature for controlling tearout and the quality of surface finish. It is present on all the planes looked at here, with the exception of the Lie-Nielsen bronze block and skew block planes. The skewed blade comes into its own when used cross-grain for jobs like fielded panels, cross-grained rebates, or trimming the cheeks of tenons, and gives a much better finish.

Tuning or fettling

I always go through the following sequence with my students, when using planes. They are essential for new Record or Stanley models, and although Lie-Nielsen planes are better quality, the flatness of the sole can still be improved – and it is worth following these steps.

Step 1

Remove the sliding front sole piece and check it over for burrs, dings or paint that might interfere with the way it seats in the body of the plane. I like to clean up the seatings with fine wire wool and metal polish,

such as Autosol, so that there is no danger of removing too much metal. This is essential to avoid the possibility of the front sole dropping further into the body after you have laboriously flattened the sole. Sometimes it is necessary to work on the seatings judiciously if there is a tendency to twist or rock – a slight twist shouldn't be too much of a problem as it will disappear when the front knob, which secures it, is tightened. It is important to note that this knob should not be over-tightened as this will distort the sole hollow in its width – in fact the setting of the tension needs to be kept consistent if the sole is to remain flat. This is a major snag on Stanley and Record planes as there is no machined support over this central area. If the fit of the front sole is sloppy from side to side, a few gentle centre punch marks may be carefully placed along the centre line of the edge, *see photo 5*. The raised bumps will cut down the slop. This technique is also useful for tightening up mitre fence guides on a table saw.

Eccentric mouth adjuster •

Blade support •

Depth of cut adjustment •

Adjustable front sole •

◄ **Throat**

◄ **Mouth**

Fig 1 Part-section through centre line of Stanley No 60½

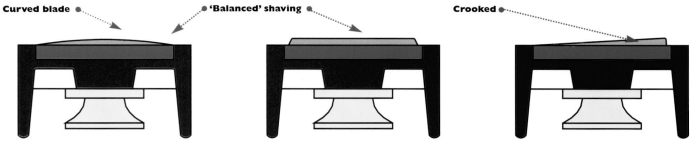

Curved blade ● ‹ · · · ·   ‹● 'Balanced' shaving ●›   Crooked ● · · · · · · · · · · ·

Fig2 Sight and adjust for a balanced shaving

Step 2

After the back of the blade has been prepared in the usual way, *(see Iron resolve, page 33)* the seating of the blade in the body can be checked. It is essential that the front edge of the blade is well supported by the machined surface at the back of the throat, *see Fig1*. This area is often found to be hollow in its width which is an invitation for chatter in the critical part of the blade. You can use engineer's blue or felt tip to reveal the contact area. A fine file can be used to correct faults, but this is an awkward operation as it is difficult to hold the file at the correct angle. I like to make a small block of wood which acts as a guide when wedged into support for the adjustment mechanism, *see photo 7*.

Step 3

The underside of the front edge of the lever cap needs to be flat in its width, in order to make good contact with the top of the blade. Often this surface is rough from the casting but is easily smoothed using some 240 wet and dry taped to a piece of MDF, *see photo 9*. The length of the lever cap is an important feature which varies considerably among different planes. Some are rather short and do not apply pressure to the blade in the relevant place. In Lie-Nielsen planes this does not happen – the blade is held just adjacent to the top of the grinding bevel, *see photo 3*.

WHICH PLANE TO BUY?

It is always a difficult problem to decide which tool to buy when there are so many makes on the market. Of the ones I have looked at here – I have not been able to include the beautiful Norris type of low-angle plane – the Stanley 60½ has always been a favourite, partly because of its narrow width –1⅜ in iron – but by the time a Hock blade has been installed the price is nearly the same as that of a Lie-Nielsen 102, which already has a thick high quality blade but no adjustable mouth.

The wider Record 60½ shown, has been subjected to a cost-cutting exercise, though like the Stanley, it can be made to work well. Its blade width is 1⅝ in.

The Lie-Nielsen 60½ is superbly made from superior materials, and has considerably more strength – and I am now a happy owner of one, and would unhesitatingly recommend them. The skew plane is very good and has no equivalent available. The No 62 is another masterpiece which is invaluable for large end-grain planing, although I do not subscribe to the view that it is good for surface planing.

All the Lie-Nielsen planes that I have examined are classics, and worth every penny. Their workmanlike beauty gives me pleasure every time I pick one up.

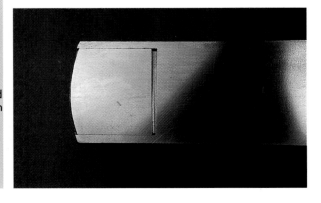

TOP: Photo 11 For planing bevels on narrow edges the plane is skewed, but pushed to and fro away from the body, not along the edge

ABOVE: Photo 12 When planing end-grain a firm two-handed grip is preferable. If the plane is skewed, the effective pitch of the blade is decreased. Less force is required and things feel smoother

BELOW: Photo 13 The 62 is capable of taking massive – 0.15 mm – shavings from end-grain. I feel this must be due to the blade thickness which is 4.5mm

Step 4

Check over all the component parts of the adjustment mechanism and ease any sharp corners which might wear away their neighbours or interfere with smooth adjustment. An example of this is the milled slot in the blade of the Lie-Nielsen models that is engaged by a disc which is integral to the stainless adjuster. Because the blade has been surface ground, the edges of the slot are very sharp.

Step 5

You will notice that Lie-Nielsen use a keyhole design for their beautiful bronze lever caps. Unfortunately when slacking off the spin wheel to make blade adjustments, it is possible for the lever cap to slide backwards depositing the contents in your lap, or worse still on the floor. Perhaps this is only due to my ineptness. However I have developed a simple modification which seems to be an improvement and solves this problem. Using the set-up shown in photo 8, a small countersunk depression can be made at the top of the keyhole. This keeps the lever cap in position and stops it sliding when making blade adjustments.

Step 6

The main screw which holds the lever cap is almost always a sloppy fit in the body casting.

This allows the screw to rock to and fro when adjustments are being made and is unhelpful. This fault is easily remedied by a few drops of Loctite nutlock, applied after the screw and hole have been de-greased. This is a form of engineering superglue which fills the voids in a loose thread, while still allowing disassembly with normal tools. But don't use bearing fit by mistake!

Step 7

You have now reached the point where the plane may be reassembled and the blade installed. As mentioned before, it is most important that the front knob, which locks the movable sole, should not be over-tightened. This will distort the sole beneath and make it hollow across the width of the plane. I usually mark the knob so that it may be reset to the same tension every time, but checking the sole with an engineer's square is more reliable.

The spin wheel on Lie-Nielsen planes should be tightened by no more than a quarter turn after the slack is taken up. The thin edge of the wedge-shaped casting, which supports the blade, could be easily damaged or cracked by over-tightening and I gather that this form of damage is often found by collectors of old planes. So with all tensions set to working positions and the blade retracted by about 2mm you can proceed with the flattening of the sole.

My current procedure is to use wet and dry stuck to 10mm (⅜in) thick float glass with a craft spray adhesive. Either water or paraffin can be used as a lubricant and it should be quite easy to see when the manufacturer's grinding marks have been removed. I usually start with about 150 grit and move through the grades with steps of no more than 100 at a time. There seems little point in polishing the base beyond 600 grit as end-grain is particularly abrasive and will scratch the metal anyway. No matter what manufacturers claim for the flatness of their grinding, castings move about and this step will always improve the performance of your plane. But it may have to be repeated again in the future.

ABOVE: Photo 14 The skew plane comes into its own for cross-grain rebating and fielded panels, as the finish is much better than that produced by a rebate plane

ABOVE: Photo 15 Sighting blade projection and balance. The illuminated white paper on the bench is a valuable aid

Step 8

Many of these planes have limited lateral adjustment available. If the blade is set in the middle of this lateral range we should see a nicely balanced blade protrusion when sighting along the sole, *see fig 2*. If this is not the case the blade grinding will need to be adjusted until it is. Precision grinding is difficult and quite large corrections may be made on an 800 grit waterstone or other coarse honing medium. It is simply a matter of applying more pressure on the side of the blade which needs shortening. With the exception of the skew blade, my preference is for a slightly curved edge in all these planes. Curved blades permit much greater control of timber removal *(see How to unwind, on page 44)*.

Step 9

With a nicely balanced, working shaving-set, you can now check whether the mouth of the plane is

even. The moving sole is closed up, and the gap between it and the blade examined. If the gap is not parallel it cannot be corrected by lateral adjustment, as this will affect the balanced working shaving. Correction is achieved by filing the front edge of the mouth to match the blade. A square filed edge, which is vertical, is fine as there is no possibility of a shaving trap. Don't be alarmed if this edge is twisted relative to the back edge of the throat, *see photo 10*. All this means is that the slope on which the blade sits is twisted relative to the sole. In a bench plane this fault is corrected by twisting the frog, a solution not available here!

All that remains is a bit of cosmetic work, easing of sharp edges – there will be one at the back of the throat – and possibly the sharp points which may appear at the front if you always use a fine mouth setting. I have seen examples where the eccentric mouth adjuster does

not have enough travel. If this is so it may be replaced by a washer or a new one made from sheet brass, *see photo 6*, my own Stanley 60½. ◼

If you are interested in taking a look at the web site mentioned in this article, it is oddly titled The Superior Works – Patrick's Blood & Gore, *and the address is:* http://www.supertool.com/Stanley BG/stan0htm.

SUPPLIERS

Axminster Power Tool Centre, Chard St, Axminster, Devon EX13 5DZ tel 01297 33656

Tilgear, Bridge House, Cuffley, Herts EN6 4TG tel 01707 873434

Bristol Design, 14 Perry Rd, Bristol BS1 5BG tel 0117 929 1740

The Craftsman's Choice, Thanet Tool Supplies, Monument Way, Orbital Park, Sevington, Ashford, Kent TN24 0HB tel 01233 501010

The Japan Woodworker, USA tel 0015 1052 11810, fax 0015 1052 11864

Karl Holtey, Unit 3, Playingfield Road, Westbury, Northants NN13 5JN tel 01280 709992 email holtey.planes@bigfoot.com

REPLACEMENT IRONS

The need for a good quality iron becomes apparent when planing the end-grain of timbers such as ebony or lignum vitae – with a standard iron the edge folds up and is shredded almost after the first shaving, unlike the better quality replacements irons which offer twice as much service.

My source for Hock irons is The Japan Woodworker in California, see left, whose catalogue is an Aladdin's cave. Ron Hock is a knife-maker and his irons are made of high carbon steel, hardened to Rockwell 62. An alternative would be old cast-steel irons from a specialist such as Bristol Design.

I also use Japanese Samurai laminated irons, which are slightly thinner, but the extra thickness of Hock irons is particularly beneficial in low-angle block planes and spokeshaves as it helps to minimise chatter.

These high quality steel irons cost nearly half the price of a bench plane but are essential for the best performance.

Perfection at a price

Comparing the delights of hand-made Norris-type planes and a more down-to-earth Lie-Nielsen

FOR THE last few weeks I have been trying out two beautiful Karl Holtey hand-made planes. They embody some of the finest craftsmanship and attention to detail that I have ever seen.

The first is based on a Norris A13 smoother, with bronze sides dovetailed to a steel sole, *see photo 1*. The handle and knob are made from old supplies of Indian rosewood (*Dalbergia latifolia*) and the blade is set at York pitch – 50° to the sole, as opposed to the Record and Stanley bench plane standard angle of 45°. The plane is nine inches long and weighs in at a hefty 5lb 9oz. The iron is thick at 4.4mm, *see photo 2*, and, combined with a fine 0.4mm mouth, has all the features required to make it ideal for final finishing of difficult, interlocked or wavy grain hardwoods.

My initial reaction on removing this plane from its green baize bag was one of astonishment and awe. Cabinetmaker friends to whom I

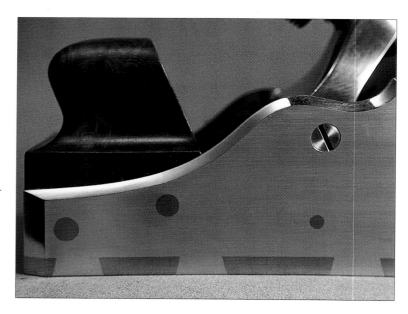

"My initial reaction on removing this plane from its green baize bag was one of astonishment and awe"

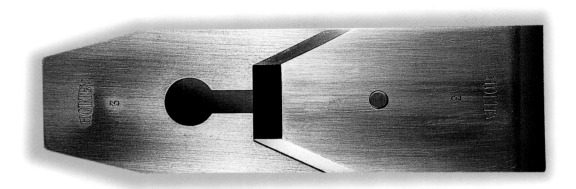

LEFT: **Photo 2 Blade and chipbreaker**

BOTTOM: **Photo 3 Smoother in use on difficult grained purpleheart**

have shown it are all equally impressed. This reaction is reinforced as familiarity with its use grows – how different to the usual experience of modern tools where more and more irritating flaws and shortcomings become apparent the closer one looks!

Blade work

Flattening of the blade's back took less time than usual, and once the sharpening was completed the heavy chipbreaker was set close to the edge and fixed. This, however, posed a slight problem; because Karl hardens the screw, it had a tendency to move the chipbreaker up the blade as it was tightened. He supplied a thin bronze washer which eliminated this irritating habit.

Blade installation requires some care as access is more restricted than in the Bailey planes with which I am familiar. This is partly due to the excellent fit of the screw head into the banjo of the Norris-style adjustment mechanism.

Before final tightening, the lever cap screw is gently

tightened and adjustments made to set the shaving and balance the blade laterally.

Karl has installed two steel 'buttons' on the inner surface of the sides, which locate the front of the blade centrally in the body, allowing accurate lateral movement at the top of the blade only – a feature not found on modern planes.

Little backlash

These are not slavish reproductions; he is constantly striving to improve his product and has taken every opportunity to study original planes, with the result that he can detect the decline of build quality in the firm's later years when the planes might have ceased to be the work of one man.

Karl is particularly proud of the positive shaving adjustment mechanism which has very little backlash. The mechanism gives a mere 20th of a turn, or 18° of backlash, whereas my Bailey planes produce about 1¼ turns.

Another nice touch is that the machine screws which fix the mechanism to the woodwork are

"This plane has a functional, pared down and workmanlike appearance providing a more subtle beauty"

tapped into a lateral brass rod concealed by the sides of the plane.

The knurling on the lever cap and adjustment knobs is another demonstration of fine detailing. Done on a milling machine to ensure crispness, apparently this is initially so sharp that some judicious blunting is required.

Lever cap

The lever cap has been produced from Karl's own pattern and is a very finely textured sand casting. He says that the finish is better than some lost wax castings that he has seen, and that he has only recently discovered a foundry capable of producing this quality of work.

This development has rekindled his enthusiasm for casting, and he is planning to extend his repertoire with more ambitious patterns. The castings are draw-filed and hand-polished so that the flatness of surfaces is not lost, as would be the case with machine-buffing.

"Karl can detect the decline of build quality in the firm's later years when the planes might have ceased to be the work of one man"

The lever cap is fixed to the body with machine screws.

Handle, knob

The rosewood handle and knob are works of art in their

own right. The front knob on this plane differs from the original; profiled on only three sides, the fourth is sloped in a similar manner to my Mathieson smoother.

The highly figured timber is flawlessly finished and the moulding is absolutely consistent. The handle is also crisply shaped; for comfort's sake, sections of the grip form various ellipses – a process which takes about three days to accomplish.

This example is finished with oil, which will develop a lovely patina with time and use.

Mitre plane

The second Holtey plane is based on an A11 Norris design – original models of this type are extremely rare and have changed hands for as much as £6,000. First impressions show it to be completely different from the smoother; the body is dovetailed in steel and has less decorative work.

This plane has a functional, pared down and workmanlike appearance, providing a more subtle beauty, *see photo 4*. These planes are principally designed for use on a shooting board so the sides are deep and without profile, affording a hard-wearing and stable base.

The massive 4.4mm thick blade is set at a low pitch angle of 20°, with the bevel uppermost, which makes it ideal for end-grain shooting. The blade is supported to within 0.8mm of the edge and the mouth is narrow.

Finger pressure

Never having owned or used a plane of this type before, I flattened and sharpened the blade with considerable excitement, and set to work.

Installing the blade requires some care, as it would be easy to blunt the sharp edge while manoeuvring it under the lever cap and onto the peg which links it to the adjustment mechanism.

This operation should become easier with a little practice.

Karl tells me that some of the original mechanisms were tilted so that the peg could be retracted below the surface of the 'stuffing' – a wooden filling – however, the tilted plane of this arrangement resulted in a lateral adjustment requiring great force.

His design does not have this fault and works with an easy finger pressure. Again, the backlash is minute, and a suitable shaving can be set with the minimum of fuss, *see photo 5*. The shooting board in the picture is no more than a simple bench hook with a layer of MDF underneath to prevent the bench from being marked. More elaborate examples are easily made.

Thin shavings were easily produced, and the stability and heft of this 6lb tool is a great improvement on my 5½ bench plane – Bailey pattern planes do not really have enough surface area on their sides and are all too easily tipped over.

Use of a shooting board is a very powerful technique, particularly useful for working on thin timber and for the production of items too small to plane conventionally.

So out of these two beautiful planes the mitre is the one for which I would be most inclined to save up.

Fine tolerances

The mechanism components, *see photo 6*, are worked to a very high standard and to extremely fine tolerances. Brass tubes, each containing a plain steel bar, act as spacers, and are fitted at every point where a rivet passes through the stuffing.

When the steel bar is riveted the spacer tube prevents movement of the filling from affecting the squareness of the sides. The stuffing on this model is leadwood (*Combretum imbrebe*), which Karl has chosen for its colour and stability. He feels that the brown tones complement the steel body, while rosewood or ebony (*Diospyrus ebenum*) are sympathetic to the bronze of the smoother. His treatment of the ends, flush and radiused, is a departure both from the original models, some of which were overstuffed with the wood emerging proud from the steel

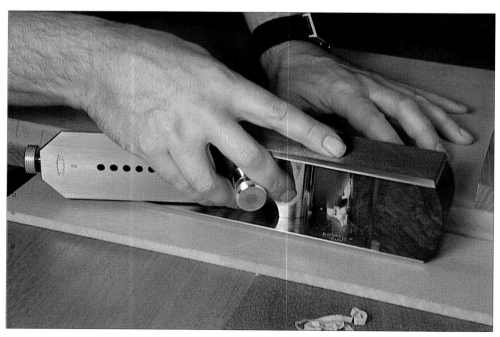

FAR LEFT: Photo 6 Mitre plane mechanism

LEFT: Photo 7 Lie-Nielsen 'Bedrock' No. 5

are works of art which function beautifully and are made to the highest standards.

Depending on the vagaries of the collectors' market – about which I know nothing – they could become a worthwhile long-term investment.

Karl Holtey charges £1,885 for his A13 smoother plane and £1,375 for the A11 mitre. He makes a range of planes based on Norris types and will also make to commission.

He can be contacted at: Unit 5, Burcote Wood Farm, Woodburcote, Towcester, Northants NN12 8TA (tel 01327 352640).

Lie-Nielsen No 5

The Lie-Nielsen Number Five, *see photo 7,* is now available in the UK through Tilgear, tel 01707 873434. Not only does it possess many desirable features, but its price ticket of £264 including VAT makes it more affordable for the average mortal.

The stress-relieved cast-iron body is heavy and well finished, with rather more substantial sides than regular Bailey planes, and unlike most planes bought today, the sides are also almost exactly square to the sole. These two factors make this 5lb 9oz plane suitable for shooting.

Based on the Stanley 'Bedrock' design, its unique frog allows for adjustment of the mouth, without removal of the blade and lever cap, *see fig 1.*

Adjustments can be made easily and precisely while working without affecting the sole.

The entire underside of the manganese bronze cast frog is machined flat, and rests on the machined surface of a wedge-shaped support which is part of the body casting.

sides, and from the sole of the Mathieson design which extends some distance from the body.

Bailey budget

I do not have shares in Holtey inc., and although this may read like a eulogy, it is only to express my admiration and enthusiasm for the fine workmanship and artistry that his tools embody.

They are, alas, well outside my budget, so I shall continue to use my tuned-up Baileys. Those who can afford a Holtey, however, will not be disappointed, for they

BUYER BEWARE

A student of mine has just spent most of a day squaring up one side of his Record No. 5½ – now discontinued. He has also suffered from an outbreak of substandard quick-acting clamps, a coping saw on which the blade could not be turned, a set of nice-looking traditional screwdrivers where not one single blade fitted the stated size of screw slot, and a precision engineer's set square with an unobtrusive lump of metal which threw it 'off' at every opportunity.

So take it from me, tool buying is a minefield for the unwary, and a great deal of time and effort would be saved if quality control were better. Caveat emptor!

ABOVE: Photo 8 Body and frog casting, showing mounting areas

How the 'Bedrock' fixing works

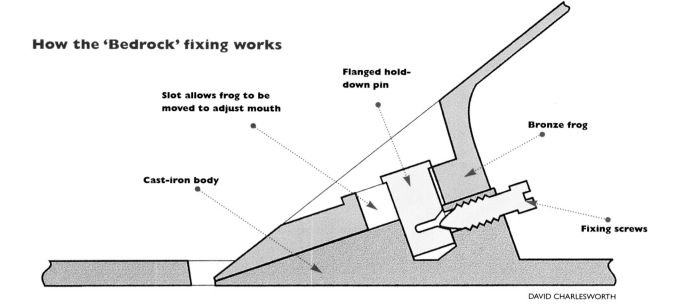

Slot allows frog to be moved to adjust mouth

Flanged hold-down pin

Bronze frog

Cast-iron body

Fixing screws

DAVID CHARLESWORTH

This mounting, *see photo 8*, is much thicker than the Bailey plane's. This critical area behind the mouth often gives problems when the frog of a Bailey play is moved, but on the Bedrock the design is improved with the provision of a solid base.

Frog fastening

The frog is held in situ by an ingenious method, *see fig 1*, by which the conical tips of two horizontal stainless steel machine screws engage slightly below centre in matching recesses in the sides of two flanged hold-down pins.

This draws the frog firmly down and locks it in place. When these screws are loosened slightly the frog may be driven forwards or backwards by the central machine screw.

The frog is a nice fit between the sides of the plane, so twisting is virtually eliminated. I feel that the absence of instructions and drawings to explain these features could be a problem for some users, however.

Some relief against choking is machined into the front edge of the mouth, though I suspect that some further attention with a file would be beneficial if the mouth were to be set very fine.

The front edge and underside of the chipbreaker would also benefit from a little work, *see Fine fettle, page 28,* but generally this plane is ready to use, and of a much higher quality than normal.

The adjustment wheel, yoke and lever cap are all of bronze;

Owing to the necessarily precise nature of the measurements stated, conversions to and from imperial and metric are not given.

the stainless lateral adjuster has a rotating disc for smooth operation. The thick 2.9mm blade is nicely surface-ground to minimise preparation time and chatter, and is equipped with a comfortable handle and knob in well-finished American cherry (*Prunus serotina*).

Conclusion

This tool is well made and very desirable, and I shall be acquiring one for the workshop and recommending it to my students. The time required to tune one up will be a cost-effective fraction of our normal routine. ■

YORK PITCH TEST

I compared the performance of the Holtey A13 smoother against my highly tuned 5½ bench plane, putting it through its paces with a piece of quartered purpleheart (*Peltogyne pubescens*) which I was told would not plane without tearout.

Both blades were freshly sharpened and the planes set up to produce extremely fine shavings of 0.02mm thick. I like to test my blade settings by taking shavings from a mild piece of scrap, measuring their thickness with callipers. Tearing large chunks out of a nearly finished piece of timber because the setting was careless is most upsetting.

The Holtey plane produced an almost flawless finish while my standard pitch plane caused considerable tearout over a wide band of interlocked timber in the centre.

Those now extremely depressed about not owning a York pitch plane may take heart: in *Scraping in,* on page 39, I describe strategies for managing perfectly well without one!

Callipers measuring shavings

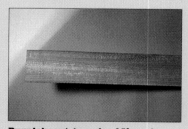

Purpleheart torn by 45° angle Bailey pattern plane

No tearing on purpleheart using 50° Holtey plane

The truth about tenons

A look at mortice and tenon joints

MORTICE AND TENONS are one of the most fundamental joints in furniture making. Tables, chairs, and frame and panel construction, are all based on this method of jointing. Tage Frid in his book, *Tage Frid Teaches Woodworking*, points out that an Egyptian sarcophagus, now in the British Museum, was framed with mortice and tenon joints at least 5000 years ago! He adds that the development of ever more complicated variations of frame and panel work in the middle ages led to the distinction between the crafts of carpentry and cabinetmaking.

Mortices

Mortices are relatively easy to cut and the number of methods available are few. Hand chopping, with a good mortice chisel, is not so difficult and produces surprisingly accurate results. Hollow chisel morticers give a consistent result if the chisel and auger bit are sharp. Routers can be used with a suitable jig and some machines allow for horizontal morticing with a slot cutter, or even an end mill.

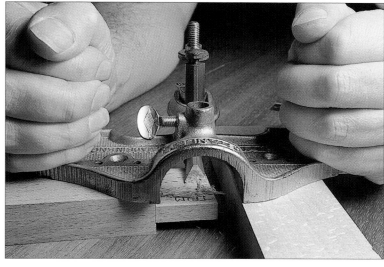

Tenons

We are then faced with the challenge of producing tenons to fit. Here the picture is entirely different and the range of available methods is bewilderingly wide. The textbooks are astonishingly silent on the subject of the practical difficulties which you may find as you strive to achieve a good result.

The usual advice is to saw directly to a gauge line and try to produce a fit straight from the saw. Some authors advocate the use of a tenon saw where the teeth have been modified to a rip pattern, while European makers prefer the bow saw. In my research I have only found one reference to a method of correcting an oversized tenon, and that was in Bob Wearing's excellent *Essential Woodworker*. This involves the use of a hand router with an offcut of the rail material screwed to the base to keep it level, *see photo 1*. This method may be easily adapted for an electric portable router, *see photo 2*.

ABOVE: Photo 1 Hand router with scrap material support used to trim an oversize tenon cheek

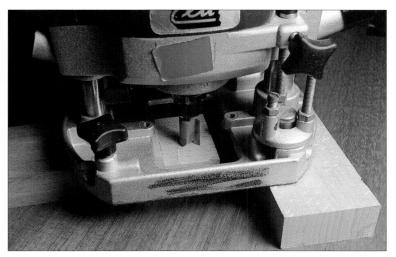

LEFT: Photo 2 Method adapted for portable router

"An Egyptian sarcophagus, now in the British Museum, was framed with mortice and tenon joints at least 5000 years ago!"

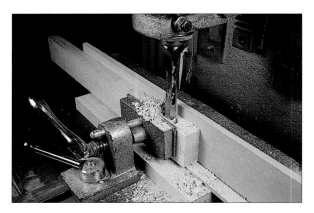

ABOVE: **Photo 3 Hollow chisel morticing – face side of stile must always be against the fence**

likely to be far from parallel and the rail is almost certainly twisted relative to the stile. The face sides are miles from flush and because you didn't correctly identify the cause of the tightness it is probably rattling about in one dimension! If this furniture-making nightmare is not familiar to you, there is little point in reading further.

Two methods

There are two methods which should avoid these frustrations. They may seem a little long-winded but should produce consistently well-fitting results. Both methods will require some scrap rail material, which has been machined at the same time as the rails, and must be of exactly the same thickness. The example described will be for a simple frame, *see fig 1* – this is for demonstration only. It would be better with a haunch to prevent twisting.

Accurate thicknessing

Accurate thicknessing of the stock is extremely important. The approach I use in the workshop is to machine the stuff very close to finished thickness, and let it settle for as long as possible.

Once the selection and orientation of the pieces are done, I hand-plane the face side and edge of each component, and then pass them

ABOVE: **Photo 5 Setting-up face side cheek cut with ruler**

twice more through the thicknesser. Once for a consistent thickness, and once for a consistent width.

Marking out is done in the normal manner with pairs of rails or stiles clamped together so that the shoulder lines and mortices are knifed at exactly the same length. This ensures that at least we will end up with a parallelogram, which is preferable to an irregular quadrilateral! Of course you don't want a parallelogram-shaped door but final clamping adjustment will pull things square.

Tenons are difficult

The truth is, that tenons are difficult, and various small errors can conspire to produce a result which is far from pleasing. You know the kind of thing – if the sawing isn't so great, you try paring a bit off the cheek, but then it's still too tight so you pare some more, but should this be from the same side? The start of the paring cuts is difficult to determine as the gauge lines have been removed when top and bottom shoulders were sawn in. Several cuts may be required as the damn thing continues to require a hammer to tap it in and you know that when glue is applied a much larger hammer will be needed. Then there is the problem of getting it apart, and much damage is inflicted when wiggling and heaving.

The cheeks of this tenon are

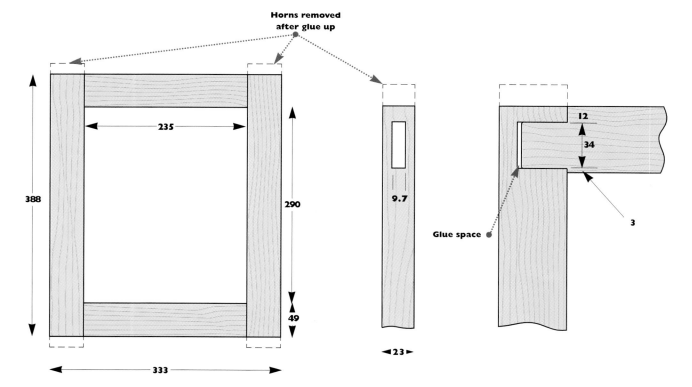

Horns removed after glue up

235

388   290   49

333

9.7

◄23►

Glue space

12   34   3

Fig 1 Frame and detail of joint

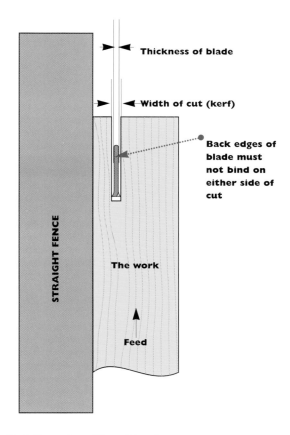

Thickness of blade

Width of cut (kerf)

Back edges of
blade must
not bind on
either side of
cut

STRAIGHT FENCE

The work

Feed

**Fig 2 Correct position of bandsaw
blade in kerf**

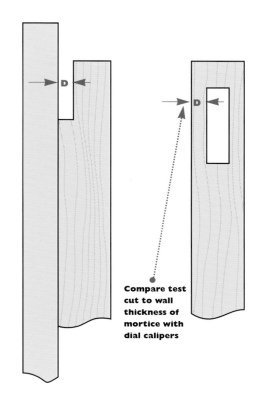

D

D

Compare test
cut to wall
thickness of
mortice with
dial calipers

**Fig 3 Method for testing
position of test cut**

Cutting mortices

Mortices may now be cut, and
the most important point to
watch is that their ends are as
consistent as possible. This is
not as easy as it sounds and
some variation does tend to
creep in at this stage. If a
morticing machine is used, the face
sides of the stiles must all be
placed against the fence of the
machine, to ensure consistency.
Failure to observe this step will
result in a door which is slightly
twisted, as it is almost impossible
to cut a mortice which is perfectly
centred in the thickness of the stile,
see photo 3.

**RIGHT: Photo 4 Checking squareness of bandsaw blade with illuminated
white paper background**
BELOW: Photo 6 Test cut for face side cheek is done first

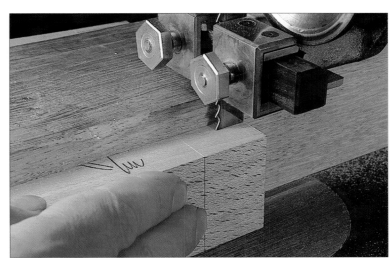

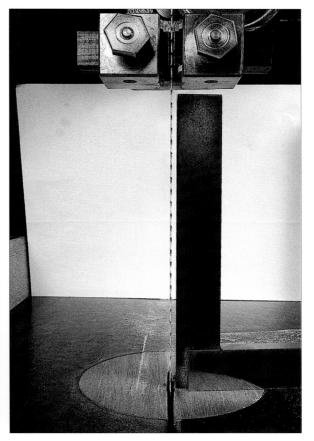

Cutting cheeks of tenons

We now come to the critical cutting of the cheeks of the tenons. These surfaces are the only part of the joint where you can expect a strong glue line, so a good fit is essential. All the other mating surfaces are composed of long-grain butting against end-grain. I always tell my students that end-grain gluing has zero strength, and while this may not be absolutely true it's not far off, unless you are using epoxy resin.

Method one

Method one relies on an accurate well set-up bandsaw, with a sharp new blade. The guides must be in

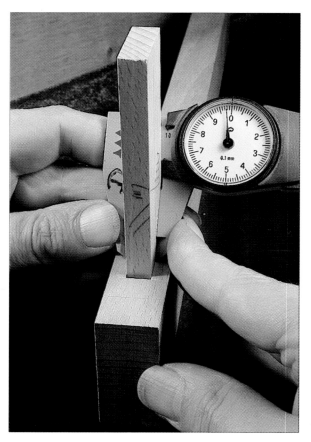

"I always tell my students that end-grain gluing has zero strength, unless you are using epoxy resin"

first rate condition with as little clearance as possible, so that the blade is not able to twist.

My Robinson Cadet has home-made Lignum vitae guides which are easy to true-up on a disc sander and may be set for zero clearance. I use a Silco blade from APTC which has very little set, and gives a good finish. If you have doubts about the accuracy of your bandsaw I suggest you follow the next steps, but cut well clear of the lines, and rely on the router table to trim to exact size. If you don't have a bandsaw, there is nothing wrong with hand sawing, except the ability of the user!

Bandsaw fence

The bandsaw fence must be set at a suitable angle to match the direction in which the blade wishes to cut. This is quite a difficult concept to explain, but when the setting is correct, the back edge of the blade should not be binding on either side of the cut, *see fig 2*. All good bandsaw fences should have provision for adjustment built in. If the set-up is not correct, the work will tend to wander away from the fence in a straight ripping cut, or the saw-cut and blade will wander off line towards the fence, trapping the work with a distinct risk of breakage. I wonder how many readers have bandsaws which suffer from this fault?

This setting becomes even more

critical when a fine set blade is used. Having no manufacturer's fence for my machine, I use a length of carefully planed timber of about 75 by 125mm (3 by 5in), as a tall fence is desirable to adequately support the face side of the work.

Next, determine whether the blade is vertical to the table. This may be ascertained by a test cut in some thick stuff, or by sighting the blade against a set square. A sheet of illuminated white paper in the background is a great help, *see photo 4*.

If you can't get everything near-perfect, at least check that the blade is reasonably parallel to the vertical edge of the fence. Again, a test cut in thick stuff will be revealing, but it must be held tight against a tall fence, rather than down onto the table.

Test cuts

Test cuts are essential if we want a good result, and hence the need for some scrap material. I prefer to make both cuts, for the cheeks, with the face side of the timber firmly against a tall fence, that is, with two fence settings, and it should ensure that the cheek surfaces are parallel. The alternative method would use one fence setting with the work being flipped.

The disadvantage of the latter method is that errors of the set-up, or timber preparation, tend to be

"If you don't have a bandsaw, there is nothing wrong with hand sawing, except the ability of the user!"

"It is the usual story, the setting up and checking has taken a considerable time, but the work only takes a few minutes!"

doubled. The advantage is that the tenon is perfectly centred. However, the mortice is unlikely to be on centre, and fence setting becomes even more critical. A fence adjustment of 0.1mm reduces the tenon thickness by 0.2mm.

Step one

Step one is to set up the face side cut, *see photo 5.* I find it best to measure from the fence to an appropriate tooth tip with an engineer's rule. This usually gives a cut which is within 0.1mm or so of the desired position. A test cut is then made in the scrap and the result carefully measured after removing some waste, *see photo 6.* Dial calipers can be used at this stage, as this measurement should be compared to the face side wall thickness of the mortice, *see fig 3.* If these figures do not agree, the fence should be adjusted and more test cuts made until they do.

Second method

The second and more reliable method is to plane up a small stick whose width is a bit less than the

length of the tenon, and ease it down shaving by shaving, until it is a nice hand fit in the mortice. When this stick is inserted in a mortice it may be compared directly with the surface of the test cut cheek, *see photo 7.* This is a very accurate method as there is no doubt about the position of the mortice.

Keep some scrap in which the final, successful, test cut was made – you will be needing it later, or better still, keep several scraps. At this stage I now make all the face side cheek cuts in all the tenons for the job. It is the usual story, the setting up and checking has taken a considerable time, but the work only takes a few minutes!

Sometimes the waste will spring due to released tension, and if there is any possibility of this holding the work away from the fence it should be removed at this stage – a hand saw, or crosscut saw being suitable.

Step two

Step two is to reset the fence for the second cheek cut. Again, with the face side against the fence, make a short test cut in the scrap piece.

When the waste has been removed, the test tenon may be offered up to the mortice on the diagonal, *see photo 8.* This is where some fine judgment is required.

Because you can only enter a corner at this stage, you can be seduced into leaving the thickness too full. When the whole tenon is finally entered, the accumulated friction may be more than you had bargained for. Two solutions are used in this workshop. The first is to measure the mortice with calipers and produce the tenon 0.1mm undersize. The better method is to compare the tenon thickness with the test stick, *see photo 9.* This is useful if the mortices have been cut by hand, as it will reveal variations before it is too late. I hate having to glue veneers to tenon cheeks, though it is a perfectly valid way of rescuing a sloppy fit.

Fence adjustment to a tolerance of 0.1mm is not easy. My final wheeze is to set the second cheek cut a fraction full. Our scrap paper is usually 0.1mm thick, so instead of attempting to move the fence, a sheet of paper or three can be placed between the fence and the work to accurately reduce the tenon thickness! *see photo 10.* I think it is worth repeating that the need for this sort of accuracy is dictated by the reality that these are the only viable glue surfaces in the joint. All second cheek cuts can now be made.

LEFT: Photo 10
Sheets of paper being used to make fine fence adjustments

BELOW: Photo 11
Length of tenon being knifed from its corresponding mortice

BOTTOM: Photo 12
Long paring chisel used to trim shoulder to knife line

"Our scrap paper is usually 0.1mm thick, so instead of attempting to move the fence, a sheet of paper or three may be placed between the fence and the work to accurately reduce tenon thickness!"

photo 2 at this stage. It is a great help if the router is fitted with a fine depth of cut adjuster as you can creep up to a final accurate dimension.

The sequence of cutting and checking is exactly the same as before, except that the work has to be flipped for the opposite cheek. One useful idea is to examine the pitch of the thread on the fine adjuster. On the Elu MOF 96, which has a 5mm metric thread, this is 0.8mm. In other words one full turn, or 60 minutes on the clock, alters the depth of cut by 0.8mm. Therefore 75 minutes on the clock represents 1mm, and 7½ minutes represents 0.1mm. This takes the guesswork out of your depth adjustment.

I have no cross slide on my router table but the arrangement shown in *photo 14* works perfectly well. It is important to hold the work firmly to the MDF support piece, but as you are taking fine trimming cuts, there should be no problem. With this method the work must be flipped over after the face side cheek has been trimmed, so a consistent result depends on accurate stock preparation.

Conclusion

It seems to have taken a long time to describe a relatively simple method, but well fitting tenons do require a careful, consistent approach. The reward should be that you spend much less time on cleaning up of the faces of the frame after gluing up. The glue-up and clamping arrangement need care and attention, as it is all too easy to twist the stiles. Clamping blocks, *see photo 15*, help to avoid this problem. ▪

ABOVE: Photo 13 Production set up to cut shoulder lines on table saw. The cut is jigged from the stop at the opposite end. Note that the perspex crown guard has been removed for clarity

BELOW LEFT:
Photo 14 MDF cross slide used to support the work on the router table

BELOW RIGHT:
Photo 15 A clamping arrangement to control the tendency of the stiles to twist

Second cheek cuts

The waste is now removed and you can attend to the cuts that determine the long dimension of the tenon. No matter how hard you try there always seems to be some variation in the length of the mortice. I like to mark each tenon with a knife as it is offered up to its own mortice, *see photo 11*.

The sawing sequence is exactly as before, but some of the cuts will need individual attention to ensure they are cut to the knife marks. Here it is equally important to ensure that the fit is not too tight – more accumulating friction! The actual fit may be gauged by offering the tenons up at an angle. This allows you to feel the fit of this dimension separately from the thickness fit.

Shoulder lines

If there is time, I prefer to remove the waste as close as possible and then cut back to the line with a razor sharp Japanese paring chisel,

see photo 12. The final cut is made by feeling the tip of the chisel drop into the knife line. Thus, if the marking out was good, the final shoulder will be in exactly the same place. It is also permissible to slightly undercut these surfaces.

In production work these shoulders would be cut straight from a table saw, with some system of stops on the mitre fence or, better still, some form of crosscutting sledge, *see photo 13*. If this is the case the rails would have been accurately crosscut to finished length before the marking out stage, as all cuts are jigged from the opposite end. In fact, with a sharp 80 tooth crosscutting blade the shoulders would probably not be marked at all.

Method two

Method two uses a simple set-up on a router table to perfect the fit of our rough cut tenons. If you don't have a router table refer back to

---

A kinder cut

Advice on cutting through dovetails with a bandsaw

LEFT: Photo I
Carcass dovetails
on John Buckham's
cherry cabinet

I WAS INTRIGUED to read an article by Paul Richardson, in which he described cutting dovetail sockets freehand on the bandsaw.

Coincidentally, my recent Australian student, John Buckham, had also been developing this technique, with impressive results, *see photo 1;* this in spite of the fact that John was able to stay for only three months and, although seriously keen, had not done any cabinetmaking before.

Dovetails have a peculiar mystique which seems to encapsulate the whole art of cabinetmaking, so if a beginner can achieve good results he or she is usually delighted.

The main requirement is the ability to saw square and to split a pencil line – one of the skills with which it is difficult to assist students. Once the basic stance is achieved, the only useful advice is to practise, practise and then do lots more.

The grip on the saw should be gentle, with the forefinger extended, and the full length of the sawblade used. The technique requires attentiveness, confidence and relaxation, and if things are not going well, the job is best left for another day.

Dovetail saw

The dovetail saw is another tool which needs fettling, even if the top of the range English product is chosen. This may be one of the best reasons to try a Japanese saw, but do take advice from a specialist as many of these are designed for softwood only.

We use a Sun Child blade for delicate work, and these are only available from Paul Brown of *The Craftsman's Choice*, tel

01233 501010. My current policy is to encourage people to try both kinds, to see which one suits them best.

A charming German student obtained two Japanese saws from a supplier in Germany, and we have proved conclusively that they don't like hard woods like Canadian maple (*Acer saccharum*). His take double the number of strokes to saw the same distance, and the kerf is not straight.

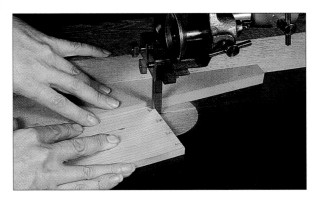

RIGHT: Photo 2 Tails being sawn on a bandsaw; note wedge to establish correct angle

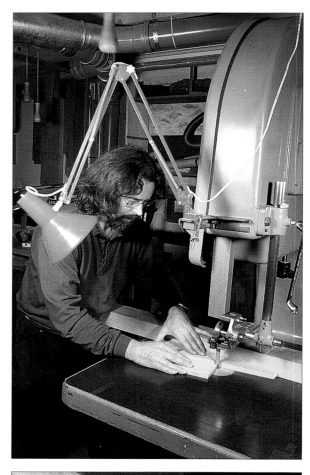

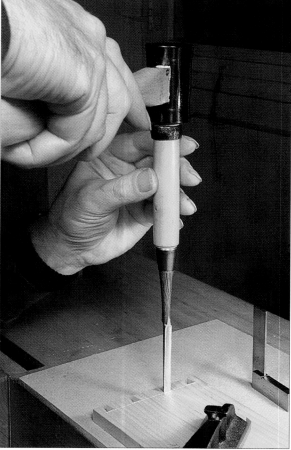

Bandsaw method

The bandsaw method is, therefore, good for those who experience trouble with sawing.

Crooked sawing is not easy to correct, so the main beauty of this approach is that the joint will always be sawn perfectly square as long as the machine table is correctly set. A pleasing result is at least halfway there.

The following anecdote relates to why I choose to saw the tails first. The story concerns two eminent and highly experienced craftsmen who in great detail explained in an American magazine why they approached through dovetailing from opposite ends. One cut the tails first and the other the pins!

My reasoning is that fine tails are almost impossible to correct if crooked, but that pins are much easier to pare if the sawing is a bit conservative. It's all very well for professionals to talk about sawing effortlessly to a line, but for most beginners this is not realistic. If beginners do not get good results fairly soon they are likely to become frustrated and disheartened.

Preparation

Just a few thoughts about preparing the bandsaw. Results will be less than pleasing if the guides are not well set to minimise potential twist of the blade. I use lignum vitae (*Guaiacum officinale*) guides which may be adjusted to touch both sides of the blade with no clearance.

The wheels are then turned over by hand to ensure that the blade is not trapped. This approach would not be possible with metal guides, where the clearance should be that of a sheet of newspaper.

The type and condition of the blade are also of the utmost importance. For all fine joint cutting we use a new, stainless, meat and fish blade, available from *Axminster Power Tools*, tel 01297 33656; ask for Silco blades. The kerf is very thin, and as the set is slight the finish is very good. They would of course be almost useless for curved cutting.

The fine set also dictates that the directional setting of a straight fence should be carefully done.

VARIETY ACT

As a design point, I prefer to vary the size of dovetails, and maybe even the pins, when they are used for carcass dovetailing. Slender pins at the edges provide more glue surfaces at the point where a carcass joint might be liable to open due to wood movement, and variation in the sizes and spacing provide visual interest and 'tension'.

> "Having the outer surface uppermost also ensures that any slight rag from the saw is on the inside of the joint"

Tails

The sockets should first be designed on paper and then marked out on the work, with a chisel-sharpened H pencil, square across the end-grain first, this being the most convenient surface for measuring.

All sorts of dovetail marking aids are available, and some work on the outside surface, obviating the need to mark the end-grain at all, as the outside surface is the one seen on the bandsaw.

Having the outer surface uppermost also ensures that any slight rag from the saw is on the inside of the joint.

Bandsawing the tails, *see photo 2*, is a simple matter. The only aids required are a correctly set straight fence and a suitable long wedge prepared to the desired slope. This long wedge – mine was a bit short – can be made from MDF or any available scrap.

The example shown has a slope of 1:6, which is an angle that we often use for through dovetails. By sliding the work up or down the surface of the wedge, fine lateral adjustments of the position of the saw cut may be made. If the first touch is a little conservative, i.e. in the waste, the work may be moved up or down the slope until the pencil line is split.

Good lighting is essential; note the Anglepoise light which is mounted on the bandsaw, *see photo 3*. This is better than fixed lighting as it provides concentrated light on one side of the blade at a time.

Don't be too ambitious about stopping exactly on the shoulder line as the bandsaw blade has a nasty habit of creeping forward about 0.5 mm at the end of a cut. This is a result of the blade's free running position, which SHOULD be that 0.5 mm clear of whatever supports the back edge of the blade in a cut.

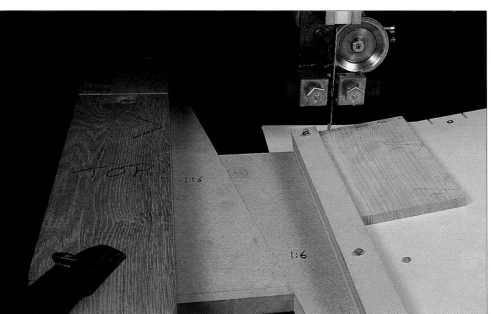

The opposite sloped cuts may be made by turning the wedge end-for-end. If the work is wide it may be necessary to adjust the fence a few times, the lateral movement of the work being limited by the length – and, therefore, width – of the wedge.

The waste may now be removed, either with multiple cuts on the bandsaw, or with a jewellers' or coping saw. My friend John Elbert has provided a good tip which makes this operation a bit less stressful, *see photo 4,* in which the mirror placed on the bench allows us to see the shoulder line on the inside surface of the work.

TOP: **Photo 6 Marking pins, made easier with a simple support piece**

ABOVE: **Photo 7 Folding wedges provide fine adjustment on this jig for sawing pins**

> "Don't be too ambitious about stopping exactly on the shoulder line as the bandsaw blade has a nasty habit of creeping forward about 0.5 mm at the end of a cut"

Jewellers' saws, with a fretsaw blade installed, are somewhat uncertain on direction of cut, so the mirror allows the body to be maintained in a steady position which would be lost if peering over the top to check progress on the back surface.

Crisp openings

Chopping to the shoulder line, *see photo 5*, is a certain and efficient method of producing crisp openings. When one of my students complained of ragged shoulder lines and showed us his paring method, the cause was immediately apparent.

For those unfamiliar with the chopping technique, the following is a description: – Select the largest chisel which will fit the socket without bruising the edges – even bevel-edged chisels usually have squarish edges.

Make some suitable mark on the blade with felt tip, Tippex or masking tape, to indicate a depth of cut which is just over half the thickness of the work. To minimise vibration, clamp the work to the bench on some scrap sheet material over or close to a leg. I prefer to sit on a low stool as this is the best position at which to judge the squareness of cut, though what is actually required is a fraction of under-cut – more is not too serious, but it is good to strive for perfection.

Several cuts may be necessary according to how much waste needs removing, but it is the penultimate and last cuts that

matter. The penultimate cuts – which are in many ways the most difficult – should be positioned to leave an even 0.25 or 0.33mm for the final cut. This minimises the wedging action of the chisel, which may bruise the line if large cuts are attempted.

It is also helpful if the shoulder line is complete so that the chisel edge may be felt and settled into it for the last cut – felt being the operative word. If the previous cut was too close, the V groove may have lost one of its sides, making the placing of the edge uncertain.

Making a cut

I like to hold the chisel near the tip to position it on the work. Then I pick up the mallet or hammer – the barrel-shaped hammer illustrated is one of my favourite tools and is, as far as I know, only available from *The Japan Woodworker,* tel 0015 1052 11810 – and give it one tap to seat the edge into the timber.

Put the hammer down again and transfer the 'grip', *see below*, to the top of the chisel with the elbow or forearm braced onto the bench. This gives good control of the vertical angle of the chisel, which may be judged against a small set square or perhaps a vertical line on a piece of scrap in the background.

The 'grip' on the chisel handle is in fact more of a gentle fingertip guide; any excessive grip is likely to twist the chisel edge out of its seating. When

satisfied with the angle, the hammer is picked up and a series of firm taps delivered until the depth of cut – just over half the thickness – is achieved.

The only point to mention here is that the elbow of the tapping arm needs to be held more or less at the height of the top of the chisel or it will be struck crooked and knocked off course.

All rough chopping is completed from both sides. Finally the shoulder line cuts may be made with a freshly sharpened chisel. To achieve a crisp, whiskerless opening, the corners must be carefully pared.

> "My other objection to vertical paring is that if it is done incorrectly, with the power coming from the forearm rather than the body weight, it is an invitation to serious tennis elbow"

As an addition to *Scraping in*, my piece on page 39 dealing with difficult grain, an interesting booklet called *Double Bevel Sharpening*, by Brian Burns, is available from The Japan Woodworker, in the U.S.A. tel 0015 1052 11810, price $9.95, in which he suggests increasing effective pitch angle of a bench plane until tearout is minimised.

I prefer to do this by horizontal paring in the vice with the aid of a good bench light, although vertical paring on the bench would also be fine for THIS part of the job.

Incidentally, my other objection to vertical paring is that if it is done incorrectly, with the power coming from the forearm rather than the body weight, it is an invitation to serious tennis elbow.

Marking pins

After a final checking, the pins can be marked out. Mark out in the usual way by tracing the tails onto the end-grain of the pin piece with a suitably delicate marking knife. The clamping aid shown in fig 5 on page 78 is considerably safer than the traditional method of balancing the wood with the aid of a plane, *see photo 6, page 67*.

For those who doubt their sawing capabilities, and who are planning to do some paring on the sides of the pins, these lines should be squared down to the shoulder line on both surfaces, with the knife.

"Fine tails are almost impossible to correct if crooked, but pins are much easier to pare if the sawing is a bit conservative"

Sawing

The sawing can now be tackled, *see photo 7*. The bandsaw method certainly worked for John, reducing the paring of the pins to a mere whisker, but I found it a trifle cumbersome.

The method is to prepare a tilted jig which supports the pin piece at the slope angle chosen for the sockets – in this example 1:6.

The surface of the jig is also fitted with a fence to support the edge of the work. To provide lateral fine adjustment to enable the sawcut to be aligned with the marking out lines, John equipped the jig with sloped edges, using another long wedge with a matching slope.

By sliding the long wedge relative to the jig, lateral movement relative to the bandsaw fence was achieved, in effect producing a pair of folding wedges, with one wedge built into the jig, *see photo 8*.

I have been wondering whether it would have been better to have a square jig, perhaps with a tilted fence and one wedge, or a straight fence and a pair of wedges. If anyone is minded to try, and arrives at a conclusion, I would be pleased to hear from them.

The waste is then removed; before chopping the final shoulder line cut, the pins may be pared to fit, *see photo 9*.

After going through this exercise, my conclusion is that bandsaw sawing of the tails is a very useful technique that is equally applicable to single lap dovetails, *see photo 10*, although I'm not so sure about its usefulness for pins. ■

LEFT: **Photo 9 Pins being pared with a long Japanese paring chisel**

DOVETAIL OR TWIST

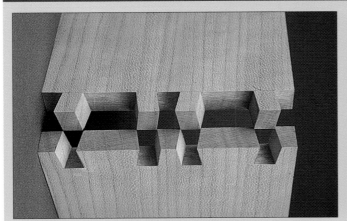

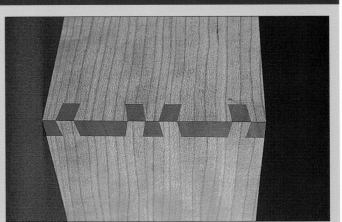

ABOVE LEFT: **Photo 11 Twisted dovetails, joint open**
ABOVE RIGHT: **Photo 12 The joint assembled**

Twist again

AS I HAVE ALREADY mentioned in *A kinder cut* (page 65), good results may be obtained when using the bandsaw to produce dovetails.

The main advantage of this technique is that the tails are sawn exactly square, which lays a good foundation for the rest of the joint.

My Robinson Cadet is an old machine, but massive and well tuned, and works well with my other secret weapon – a very fine, stainless frozen meat and fish blade sold by APTC as "Silco". The kerf sawn with this is about 1mm wide and it leaves a smooth finish as the set is minimal.

Secret

Once the joys of working with a well-set up bandsaw have been experienced, the intrepid dovetail-user will realise that any variation of the joint may be cut in the same way – providing that the nature of the joint is understood and suitable jigs are made. The twisted dovetail is an interesting variant, and here I propose to describe my method

for producing this unusual and fascinating joint.

The secret of this joint is that it may only be assembled by offering the inner corners up and driving them together at 45 degrees; easier said than done, *see fig 1*. The same procedure is used in reverse to disassemble.

In order for this to work the slopes used on the tongues MUST be the same angle on both surface and end grain. This should be clearly visible in photo 2.

ABOVE: Photo 1 – A Twisted Dovetail
LEFT: Photo 2 – The two halves of the joint

Variables

The origin of this joint appears to be in Japan.

Alan Peters has described it, in *Fine Woodworking* magazine, and says that he was shown it by a visiting Japanese student whose name for the joint is *nejiri arigata*.

In fact, the only time that I have ever seen it used was in a fine yew (*Taxus baccata*) coffee table which Alan exhibited at the Devon Guild Of Craftsmen's summer exhibition some years ago.

Gustav, a Swedish journeyman student who spent some time in my workshop not long ago, showed me how it was done – he

"The number of variables has clearly exceeded four and my brain is beginning to hurt"

If life has become too straightforward, try a compound dovetail joint

in turn was taught the joint by a Japanese fellow student at the Karl Malmsten School.

I have never seen the joint described in a book.

The design possibilities are numerous as the joint has four main elements which may be varied.

The twin, parallel, part whose function is similar to the pin of a through dovetail, will be referred to here as the 'tongue'. Moving from left to right on fig 2a the space between the first two tongues is a dovetail shape so it will be called the 'tail'.

The next space will be called a 'reverse tail'.

The angle chosen for the tongue may be varied in the normal way, perhaps between 1:5 and 1:8 as for conventional dovetails. The width of the tongue, tail and reverse tail may all be adjusted to give various visual effects.

There is also no reason why alternate tongues should reverse their slope and, as a final thought, the angle of successive tongues need not always be the same, *see fig 2c*.

This is becoming very Pythonesque, as the number of variables has clearly exceeded four and my brain is beginning to hurt.

Marking out

Marking out for the bandsaw method is delightfully simple, as it may be done on the outside surface of one piece only, in pencil.

I chose to mark the socket piece first, but am fairly sure

"My gauge setting was a bit oversize which caused me a lot of trouble when it came to clamping the joint for glue-up"

that the pin piece could equally well be chosen. The timber should be carefully thicknessed – all pieces the same – and true, square ends shot, perhaps with the aid of a bench hook.

Face sides are internal, and face edges should all be aligned on one edge of the carcass. A suitable gauge is set to a fraction less than the thickness of the timber and used to mark the shoulder lines from the ends.

On the face side, we may mark right across the width except for the first and last 5mm or so. On the reverse – which will be the outside – we mark only where the waste is to be removed.

Incidentally, my gauge setting was a bit oversize which caused me a lot of trouble when it came to clamping the joint for glue-up, and explains the cardboard pressure pads in the clamping arrangement photo.

ABOVE: Photo 3 – Sawing openings on the bandsaw
BELOW: Photo 4 – Waste removed by multiple sawcuts

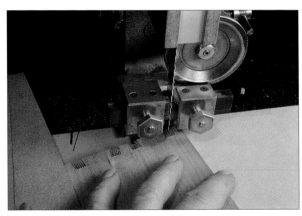

BELOW: Photo 5 – View of sloped jig

DOVETAIL PROPORTIONS

I prefer to do all the design of proportions on paper, mainly by sketching. When the appearance begins to look reasonable it is necessary to do some measuring and arithmetic – it is also wise to consider the size of available chisels.

This may be a slow approach, but it has the advantage of making one look at the proportions and consider whether they are pleasing to the eye. Traditional rules are sometimes a bit stultifying, and there is nothing more disappointing than the 'half pin' on a drawer front that has been planed away in the fitting until it looks skinny and fragile.

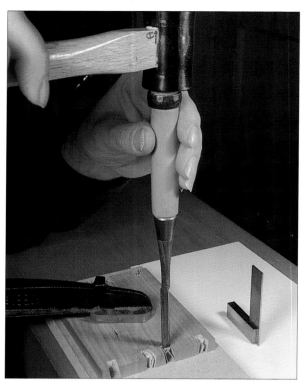

LEFT: **Photo 7a – Chopping the shoulders**
ABOVE LEFT: **Photo 7b – Completing the cut to the shoulder line**
ABOVE RIGHT: **Photo 7c – Horizontal paring to clean the lumps from the corners**

> "I didn't have time to make another as I was off soon for my annual ski trip"

Socket jig

Sawing the sockets on the bandsaw was done with the same jig which John Buckham made for the pin half of his bandsawn through dovetails, *see A kinder cut,* page 65.

I didn't have time to make another as I was off soon for my annual ski trip.

This worked well but is not ideal; you will see a rather

CLAMPING PROBLEMS

Closing this joint, at 45 degrees, is not easy so I decided to use a clamping arrangement similar to the one used for mitres and secret mitre dovetails, see *photo 11 and fig 1*.

In this case it was not convenient to glue clamping blocks to the work, so instead they were glued to thin plywood which was then clamped to the work.

ABOVE: **Photo 11 – Clamping procedure with new Bessey clamps**

ABOVE: **Photo 12 – Disassembly with folding wedges**

This worked fine, but disassembly might pose a problem if you wish to have a dry run at the glue-up first. My solution was to screw slightly longer sticks to the sloped surface of the clamping blocks, allowing the protruding ends of these sticks to be forced apart in the correct direction with pairs of folding wedges, see photo 12.

I know that this all sounds rather involved but it is worth taking great care with gluing – we have perhaps 10 or 15 minutes before the glue begins to set and it is easy to wreck days or even weeks of work if things go wrong.

The Bessey clamps shown are relatively new. Their advantage is that the jaws remain parallel as the clamp is tightened, rather like wooden handscrews. This was a great help in this case as the universal ball joint of a conventional G-clamp might well have tipped off the narrow surface of the stick.

Fig I – Blocks screwed to ply are essential to enable the two pieces to be drawn together

Direction of assembly

Ply

Cramping pressure

Sticks to aid disassembly

Clamping blocks

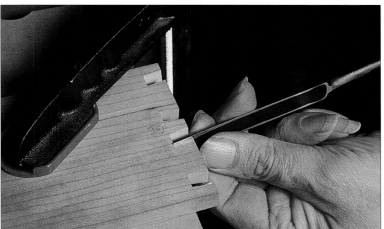

cumbersome arrangement in photo 4 where two 1:6 wedges are being used against the fence on the jig.

All that is really needed is a surface tilted at the chosen tongue angle – this would need to have parallel edges so that it may be reversed and a fence fixed to the surface, parallel to the edges, *see fig 3*.

With such a jig it would only be necessary to use one 1:6 wedge to tilt the work left or right

on the surface.

Incidentally, before the sawing of the openings is begun it is worth being absolutely clear about which way each sawcut slopes on the end-grain. This marked-out surface is not seen when cutting on the bandsaw and as half slope one way and half the other the scope for an error is significant.

I used a simple code on the top surface to avoid mistakes. The temptation to flip the work over

was also resisted, as there is a slight rag on the exit side of the sawcut which is best confined to the interior of the joint.

When everything is in nearly the right place, fine lateral adjustment of the work is made by advancing or retracting the wedge – so the wedge should be quite long. Using this technique it should be quite easy to split the pencil lines, *see photo 4*.

As a slight variation, multiple cuts were made with the bandsaw to remove most of the waste from the openings – in *A kinder cut* (page 65) a jewellers saw was used for this.

Clean up

The shoulder lines were then cleaned up by chopping with a chisel and hammer, or mallet for European chisels. Slightly undercut surfaces are produced by cutting half way through from each side.

During this operation the bench top is protected by some suitable sheet material, and the work is clamped near a leg to minimise vibration, *see photo 7a*.

Almost all chisels have a nearly square edge which will bruise the sides of the openings, so choose a slightly narrower chisel. This will leave small lumps in the corners, which will have to be dealt with.

I have recently honed a 1:6 angle on the edges of a 6mm chisel for this purpose. It was hard work and took some ingenuity to dream up a suitable jig, but the results have been pleasing, *see photo 8*.

Fig2 – Some design possibilities for twisted dovetails

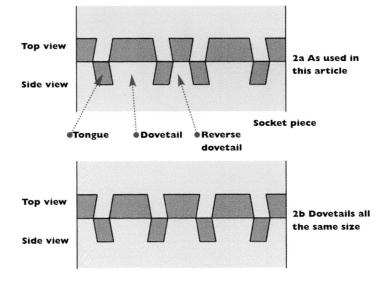

Pin piece

Top view

Side view

2a As used in this article

●Tongue   ●Dovetail   ●Reverse dovetail

Socket piece

Top view

Side view

2b Dovetails all the same size

Top view

Side view

2c Sunburst arrangement

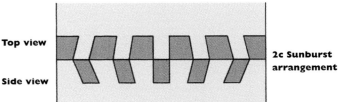

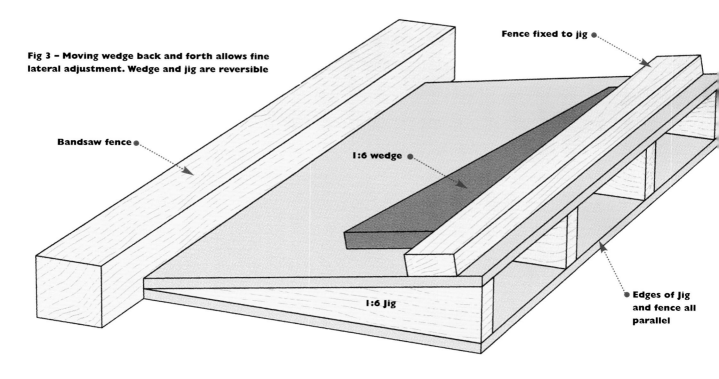

Fig 3 – Moving wedge back and forth allows fine lateral adjustment. Wedge and jig are reversible

Fence fixed to jig ●

Bandsaw fence ●

1:6 wedge ●

1:6 Jig

● Edges of Jig and fence all parallel

The Editor tells me that he has always used a straight bladed knife for this job, and it is also possible to use an undersized chisel – slightly skewed so that the edges do not bruise the sides. This topic seems to be interesting and I would welcome readers' views.

In this example the bandsawing did not quite reach the shoulder line, so I completed the cut with a chisel, *see photo 7b*. It is OK to just cross the shoulder line as the excess cut will close up again later.

This is the only time I ever attempt a cut in the direction of the wood fibres – it only works because the cut is so short, perhaps half a millimetre, but has the effect of separating the fibres thus making the lump in the corner easier to see and remove, *see photo 7b*.

Because the cut in line with the grain is slightly too deep, the lump will fall away when correctly severed at the roots! I strongly advocate this principle, as scraping around with a chisel is a serious abuse of the edge.

Knife line

Contrary to what you may have read elsewhere, the second half of the joint may be marked directly from the first.

It took a while to figure this out and the method is shown in Photo 9; here the socket piece is stood on top of the other half and the openings traced onto the end grain with a hobby knife or scalpel – note that the two pieces are in the same plane.

These lines were then knifed down to the shoulder line with a small sliding bevel.

Demon sawyers amongst you might prefer to do this in pencil, but I was planning to do a little paring on these surfaces and a knife line affords a good seating for the start of the cut. Paring to a pencil line seems a little uncertain to me.

All the cutting and finishing procedures for this half are similar to those already described, with the exception of the edge shoulders. No undercutting is required here and great care is needed to produce a tight fitting result.

The importance of checking each surface cannot be overstated. Over the years I have noticed a general reluctance amongst my students to perform this task – perhaps it is our enthusiasm to see the finished result.

Are the cut surfaces flat? Were they cut crisply to the line? Were the lines marked in the right place anyway? Great damage may be inflicted by forcing an overtight joint together in a hurry.

This inspection phase also provides clues to remedying deficient technique, poses an intellectual challenge and encourages Sherlock Holmes fantasies!

Only when satisfied that all is well should you proceed to the gluing-up stage, see panel.

The result of this exercise may be seen in photo 1.

I was pleased with the results and my solution to this puzzling joint – the only remaining riddle is to think of some suitable furniture applications! ■

**TOP: Photo I
Mitred edge allows
mouldings to be
cut in**

Uncovering the secret

The dreaded secret mitred dovetail
is easy (ish)!

THE SECRET mitred
dovetail is one of my
favourite joints; I prefer
cutting these to making through
dovetails, although they are a
little laborious.

At first sight they appear to be
more complex, but analysis
reveals only two surfaces on each
half that have to fit perfectly,
whereas a through dovetail may
show errors on
two surfaces, each
sawcut therefore
having to be
virtually perfect.

I have many
skilled
cabinetmaking
friends, and they
all say that on a
good day their
dovetailing is OK
– they tend to be
a modest lot – but
we all have off days when the
results are slightly disappointing.

So, to those who can cut
respectable single lap dovetails,
secret mitre dovetails will not
pose too much in the way of
difficulty, and the results will be
extremely satisfying.

Visual effects
This joint has several uses in
high quality work, such as
plinths, boxes and carcasses,
where strength and appearance
are important. It is also valuable
for veneered work, through
which ordinary dovetails would
ghost.

The Makepeace workshop
appears to be using them for fine
drawers, producing a smart result
in which the grain and figure

> "Please note that
> this is the one
> form of dovetail
> where the pins
> must be marked
> and cut first"

flow around a corner in an
uninterrupted manner.

This interesting visual effect is
also present on the edges,
allowing neatly mitred mouldings
to frame the opening, *see photo
1*. The aesthetics of a piece will
be completely different if
through dovetails are chosen.

Marking out
As with most
operations, it is
wise to lay out the
pins on paper at
full size before
starting work.
Finding that the
shoulder line to be
pared is one
millimetre smaller
than the smallest
available chisel is
infuriating.

In the example
shown, *see fig 1*, the narrow pins
at either edge are there to provide
two glue surfaces near to the
mitred edge, so preventing gaps
appearing later.

Even at this size I had to use a
4.5mm chisel to chop the waste
from the socket. This has raised
the question of terminology. I
prefer to refer to pins and sockets
– the hole into which the pin
goes – as both parts are of a
dovetail shape.

The mitred section at either
side is usually about 6mm (^{1}/4in)
wide, but must be of sufficient
size to accommodate any planned
moulding of the edge.

Light scratch
I have cut this joint in members
of differing thickness, but

obviously the angle of the mitre
then ceases to be 45°. The usual
method is to start with accurately
thicknessed stuff, the ends being
shot or planed square.

Set a cutting gauge to the
timber's exact thickness, with the
flat side of the blade facing away
from the stock, and mark the
shoulder line S1 on the face –
inside surface – of each piece.
Most of this line should be
deeply scored, but I think it helps
if the ends are only lightly
scratched, *see fig 2*.

A mitre square or adjustable
bevel may then be used to knife
in the mitres on the edges. This
operation requires good light and
great care as it is critical to final
success; small errors here lead to
tedious fitting and adjusting at a
later stage, thus the light scratch
at the edges – a knife line can be
surprisingly wide.

Incidentally, I never trust mitre
squares, squares or adjustable
bevels with wooden stocks;
WEZU manufacture two
affordable engineers' mitre
squares, available from
Axminster Power Tools.

Lap L thickness
The thickness of lap L should
have been decided at the design
stage. We usually use a figure
which is between a third and a
quarter of timber thickness T; too
thin and the dovetails may ghost
through to the outside of the job,
too thick and the glue area of the
pins is being unnecessarily
reduced.

Set another cutting gauge –
same orientation as before – to T-
L and gauge across the end grain

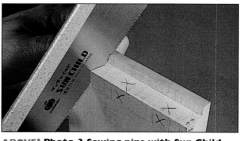

ABOVE: Photo 2 Template used for pin marking

ABOVE: Photo 3 Sawing pins with Sun Child blade

ABOVE: Photo 4 Paring cut to complete sides of pins

ABOVE: Photo 5 Using mitre guide block

ABOVE: Photo 6 Some waste being chiselled from lap

ABOVE: Photo 7 Marking the sockets using the support piece

from the face side.

This line is also taken down the edges until it just meets the mitre line. A third cutting gauge is now set to (D + 0.1mm); this is my own variation, D being the distance from the end to the intersection previously mentioned.

This gauge is used to mark the rebate which must be cut in the ends before the pins are marked out.

Here is the dilemma: if the rebate is cut shy of the lines the joint will be held open, as will the inner shoulder line at the junction of the two face sides; if the rebate is cut just past the lines the mitre on the edge will be nicked.

Crosscut blade

My solution is to cut well up to both lines, but not quite to full depth, using a crosscut blade in the table saw. I have a nasty suspicion that this may now be illegal, as it requires that the blade is unguarded, so perhaps a safer alternative would be to use a straight cutter, router table and fence, cutting in from both directions.

Anyway, the result is a small lump left in the corner of the rebate, *see fig 3*, which is now chiselled away from the centre section where the pins are to be marked out, but not from the extreme edges.

Please note that this is the one form of dovetail where the pins must be marked and cut first.

Home-made template

In readiness to mark out the pins,

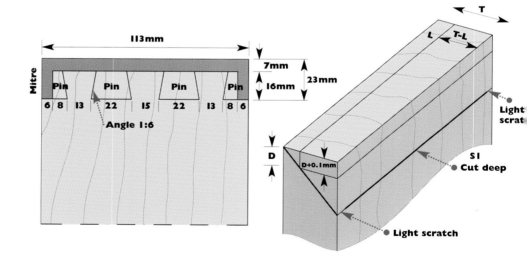

Fig 1 The pin layout

Fig 2 The ends should be only lightly scratched

a home-made template of brass or very hard wood is required, *see photo 2*. This is double-ended with parallel edges; an angle of 1:6 is suitable for hardwoods.

The marking out is done on the end-grain; I prefer to do it with a knife as the joint is completed by paring the sides of the pins. For

those who are good at sawing, pencil might suffice, and this method is undoubtedly quicker.

The square lines for the outer surface of the edge pins can be marked using the true end of an engineers' steel rule.

All these lines are now squared down with a knife to the

ABOVE: Photo 8 Paring majority of waste from the long mitre, using paper to control cut

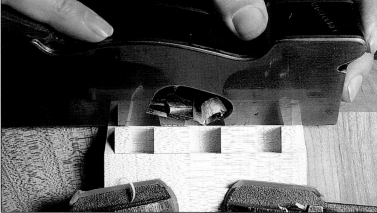

ABOVE: Photo 9 Support block and shoulder plane used to finish long mitre

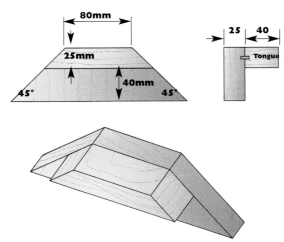

ABOVE: Fig 3 A small lump is left in the rebate

ABOVE: Fig 4 A homemade mitre guide

"The end sockets must be completed before the mitres of the socket pieces are sawn off"

shoulder line S1, using a small square; the waste is marked with pencil.

The waste can now be sawn and chopped from between the pins, one paring cut inside the knife lines and the saw held at about 45°. Nicking the lap is of little consequence, but do not cross the far top edge.

Go to finished depth with each cut when chopping out the waste. I use masking tape on the chisel as an depth-indicator, with MDF or ply to protect the bench top. Chopping with a mallet or chisel hammer is best done above a bench leg to reduce vibration.

Rough out all these recesses to within one chisel cut of the line, then resharpen all the chisels before finishing to the knife and gauge lines.

More chisels

A pair of skew-ground chisels is useful for ridding all recesses of whiskers, *see panel*. For a method of paring the sides of the pins, *see photo 4*.

The final cleaning up cut is greatly assisted by the use of a long paring chisel which makes control and judgment of the angle much easier, *also see panel*. The pin piece of the end mitres may be sawn in next with the aid of a home-made mitre guide.

Any undercutting here will show on the long mitred edge and also on the internal shoulder

line, *see photo 5* and *fig 4*. An upward rotational movement of the chisel handle achieves the interesting paring of the outer pin surface.

A useful aid to marking out sockets is to clamp the pin piece vertically to a support piece fixed to the bench top, with its face side exactly on the shoulder line of the socket piece, *see fig 5*.

After the face edges have been aligned, *see photo 7*, this is also clamped to the bench. Nothing must move until the pins have been traced onto the socket piece.

Feeling a chisel edge into a scalpel line is a difficult procedure, but a Swann-Morton craft knife has a blade of an appropriate thickness. Whatever knife is used, the angle at which it is held is critical.

Setting up a bench light to view the 'tracing' is helpful, *see panel*, as big trouble will follow if a line that goes astray is not corrected immediately.

The end sockets must be completed before the mitres of the socket pieces are sawn off. The traced lines are now squared down to the shoulder line S1 as before and the waste marked.

Sawing, chopping and paring are completed as before, with one minor variation; run some square sawcuts to allow the waste to escape without knocking the corners off the dovetails.

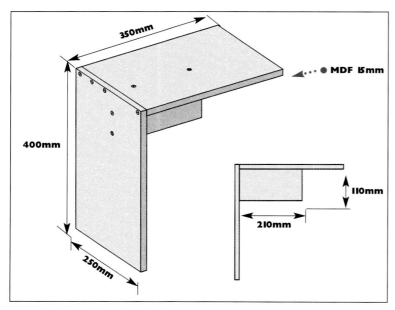

ABOVE: **Fig 5 A useful aid for marking out sockets**

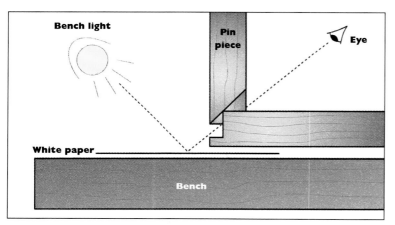

ABOVE: **Fig 6 Checking fit of pins**

Checking work

Checking every surface of the joint is imperative – and fundamental to improving work. Craftsmanship is more concerned with method and attitude of mind than some intrinsic magical skill, so the checklist should include questions like: Are the glue surfaces flat or bumpy? Is the chopping of the shoulder line square or slightly undercut? Are there lumps or whiskers in the corners? Did those paring cuts split the knife line?

Proceed when the answer to all these questions is 'yes'.

The pins should enter by about a third; if they don't, make any obvious adjustments. Now the socket mitres can be sawn off; pare to the line using the mitre guide, checking that they meet

the shoulder line scratch S1 exactly.

Long mitre

An aid to finishing the long mitre on the lap is made from quartered accurately surfaced timber preferably a few inches wider than the job. A true mitred end is prepared with sawbench, plane and straight-edge, *see fig 7*.

This is clamped to the work with the previously pared end mitres accurately aligned with its sloping surface. Judicious tapping with a small hammer is a great assistance here.

The majority of waste may now be chiselled away, *see photo 8*. For the final few paring cuts place sheets of paper under a broad paring chisel, applying a lot of pressure on the chisel

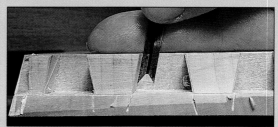

ABOVE: **Photo 4A Skew chisel being used to clean out corners**

QUALITY JAPANESE sawblades – see *photo 3* for the best affordable example that I have found to date – are available from The Craftsman's Choice, tel 01233 501010. Because slightly inferior Japanese tools are available in this country I advise going to a specialist like Paul Brown of the above-mentioned establishment.

No, I do not own shares, but I am very enthusiastic about good tools and good books. Besides the sawblades, I also cannot recommend highly enough the various Japanese chisels being used in the photos.

Opinions vary on the subject of edge hardness. My own view is that for work involving paring or chopping the end grain of abrasive hardwoods, there is no comparison between the performance of Japanese or modern English chisels, which are not hard enough. My experience tallies with that of James Krenov and Jim Kingshott, in that the Japanese variety is not more difficult to sharpen.

I can see no reason to spend much money on skew chisels, see *photo 4A*. The two elegant cast-steel chisels, see *photo 4B*, were found in a local market for £8 the pair. A fair amount of work had to be done to flatten the backs, but the grinding and sharpening is not difficult.

The main problem with old tools tends to be rust pitting deeply into the flat side, necessitating the removal of much metal. Beware also of a badly convex back, the result of years of sharpening on a hollow stone and almost impossible to eliminate.

The long, thin-bladed, Japanese paring chisels are a favourite with all my students and are available from Thanet tools or The Japan Woodworker.

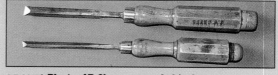

ABOVE: **Photo 4B Skew-ground chisels**

above the paper. This controls the cut and stops the chisel diving.

In this manner a minimum of timber is left to be removed with a razor-sharp wide shoulder plane, *see photo 9*.

Plane from both edges to stop the tool from splitting out the edges, and do not remove timber

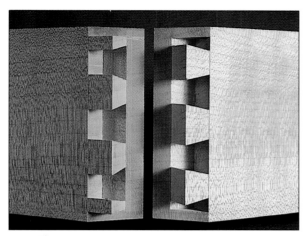

ABOVE: **Photo 10 The finished joint halves**

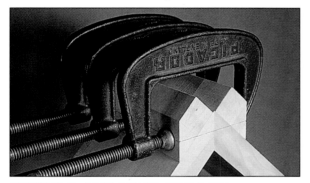

ABOVE: **Photo 11 Glue blocks and G clamps to close the mitre**

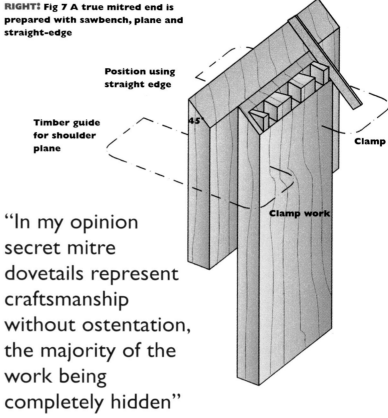

RIGHT: **Fig 7 A true mitred end is prepared with sawbench, plane and straight-edge**

Position using straight edge

Timber guide for shoulder plane

45°

Clamp

Clamp work

> "In my opinion secret mitre dovetails represent craftsmanship without ostentation, the majority of the work being completely hidden"

from the previously cut end mitres. The aim is to plane a flat surface (checking with a straight edge) which mates exactly with them.

Avoidance strategies

Various strategies can be adopted to avoid planing the surface of the guide block. In *The Technique of Furniture Making* Joyce advocates wax, and I have had success with Magic Sellotape taped over the sole and blade where a cut is not desired. Possibly the best solution is adjusting the blade so that it only shows where the cut is wanted.

RIGHT: **The closed joint**

Finished halves

I had a narrow escape from an over-enthusiastic sawcut, *see photo 10,* of the finished joint halves, but I am proud to say that the joint went home first time with a few gentle taps from a medium-sized hammer.

Do check that the boards are square during assembly and disassembly as nothing does more damage then wiggling a joint when trying to take it apart by hand; a big hammer, some scrap and a set square are the right tools for the job.

Gluing up

Purpose-made glue blocks are the key to successful gluing up. A sad fact is that joints which behaved immaculately at the dry glue-up stage have a nasty habit of turning 'ornery' once the glue is applied.

These blocks should be made of accurately prepared hardwood, and may be glued to the work if it is solid. If this is not desired, try fixing them to thin ply or MDF and clamping the result to the work.

The flat tops

allow sash cramps to be used to drive the pins home. Small G clamps may be used to close the long mitre, *see photo 11.*

In my opinion secret mitre dovetails represent the best of craftsmanship without ostentation, the majority of the work being completely hidden. ■

PUTTING LIGHT ON THE SUBJECT

A BENCH light may be used to assess fit. Placing a sheet of white paper on the bench and offering up the pins to the socket, *see fig 6,* will provide a fair idea of the 'tracing's' fit, and whether any adjustments are necessary.

A hairline of light should be visible when the eye is lined up with the plane of each joining surface; no light means too tight and recourse to a big hammer is likely to split something.

Tricks with tapers

Using a router to produce tapered dovetail housings

"HOW WOULD you like to write about tapers in the workshop?" the Editor suggested. Concluding that this covered a vast field, I decided to concentrate on a router method for producing the interesting dovetail housing joint, *see fig 1*.

One textbook, *Tage Frid Teaches Woodworking*, warns that it is only likely to come right after you have goofed up about a dozen times.

This tricky joint may be considered for two reasons. The first is that in solid wood a plain or single-shouldered housing has very little effective gluing area, relying almost entirely on friction and a good fit as all the glue surfaces are end-grain to long-grain.

A dovetail housing has the advantage of providing a mechanical link between the sides of tall carcasses or bookshelves, preventing the sides from bulging outwards under load.

The second reason applies when a shelf may have to be slid from the back into a deep carcass which has bowed in its width since thicknessing. The

cumulative friction and swelling due to moisture in the glue conspire to make assembly well nigh impossible, spelling ruination for the job.

Tests and tools

The taper allows the shelf to enter easily, and not tighten up until it is almost home, but, because Sod's Law may still prevail, several test joints must be made with scrap. Glued up at leisure, these may reveal that a joint which enters fully when dry still stops 10mm short when glued, depending on the taper angle and the choice of glue, *see panel*.

A tenon saw, chisels and a router plane will suffice to make this joint by hand, but a side rebate plane, like the Record 2506S, may be an advantage. Even the router plane may be replaced by a suitably ground concrete nail in a block of wood. This may then be used to scrape down high spots in the base of the housing to form a flat base.

I am highly entertained by the number of sophisticated and desirable looking tools which are appearing on the market to address problems which a shop-

> "The problem-solving element of furniture-making is one of its most satisfying aspects"

made tool will deal with for a few minutes' work.

The problem-solving element of furniture-making is one of its most satisfying aspects. These comments are NOT aimed at the excellent and versatile router plane. I do not propose to describe the hand technique as it is well described in both Ernest Joyce's *Furniture Making* and by Frid.

Marking out

All joints should be drawn out on paper with a sharp 2H pencil before the timber is marked. The initial shaping is done with a chisel or knife and involves putting long, shallow slopes on opposite sides of the pencil to produce a square-ended tapering lead, *see fig 2*.

Fig 1 Dovetail housing joint

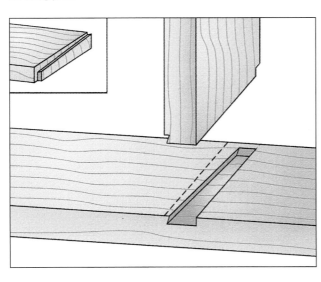

> "A dovetail housing has the advantage of providing a mechanical link between the sides of tall carcasses or bookshelves"

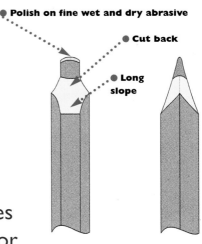

● Polish on fine wet and dry abrasive

● Cut back

● Long slope

Fig 2 A precision sharpened 2H pencil will draw a line of negligible thickness

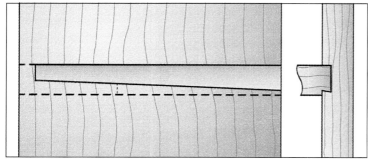

Fig 3 Housing in carcass side stopped 10mm from front edge

"Too much taper will weaken the load-bearing capability of the shelf, so angles measured in degrees are not meaningful in this exercise"

The wood at either side may be cut back a bit and the final shape worked on two grades of fine wet and dry — 400 grit for shaping and 1000 grit for polishing; or 400 grit may be blunted by rubbing the two sides alternately with a circular motion and a slight rocking of the wrist, to produce a crescent-shaped edge.

The thickness and width of the shelf and the thickness of the carcass side are now drawn out. The depth of housing can be about a third of carcass thickness, and in this case I made it 5mm deep, *see fig 3*.

If the joint is to be machine-cut two router cutters will be needed. The straight cutter must be the same or a smaller diameter than the 'neck' of the dovetail cutter, *see fig 4*. This neck dimension is affected by the depth of cut. Suitable router cutters for small work are not numerous.

The traditional angle for hand-work is about 10°, and I ended up with a TL 70 bit from the Grade Router Cutter catalogue (Grade Router Cutters, formerly trading as Griffiths, tel 01633 266481) — 8° with a base diameter of 9.5mm (3/8in).

When used at 5mm depth the neck diameter is 8.1mm so an 8mm diameter straight cutter is employed, but a greater depth of housing would call for a smaller diameter cutter, so avoiding removal of the top of the sloped face.

The narrow end of the housing surface must be wider than the neck diameter of the dovetail cutter, by at least the undercut of the dovetail bit, which is about 0.7mm in this example. If it is not, the square edge of the housing will be undercut by the dovetail cutter.

These considerations allowed me to use a simple dado jig, positioned only once, to produce the housing. The method allows accurate repeatability, but there are of course alternatives.

Another tip is to use two routers, both guided by the same diameter guide bush, in this example 14mm outside diameter. This simplifies the machining as cutters do not need to be swapped over and the depth of cut does not need constant resetting.

Calculating ratio

The ratio of the taper along the length of the housing and the width at the back and front edge of the carcass must now be decided.

Usually the housing will be stopped short of the front edge, say by about 10mm. Width of housing at the back edge might be 3mm less than shelf thickness, to provide some shoulder.

In hand-work the taper over the length is usually about 3mm (1/8in) as well, but for some obscure reason the taper chosen for this example was 4:100, and one could argue that the 'tongue' at the front is a bit thin.

Too much taper will weaken the load-bearing capability of the shelf, so angles measured in degrees are not meaningful in this exercise, when it is much easier to lay out a taper in terms of height gained over a distance travelled, like the old gradient road signs for steep hills.

Any convenient units may be used and only a ruler and a set square are needed.

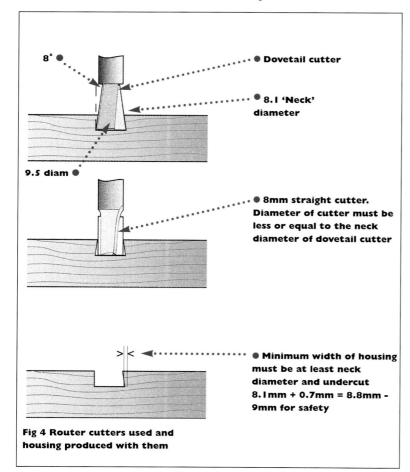

8°

9.5 diam ●

● Dovetail cutter

● 8.1 'Neck' diameter

● 8mm straight cutter. Diameter of cutter must be less or equal to the neck diameter of dovetail cutter

● Minimum width of housing must be at least neck diameter and undercut 8.1mm + 0.7mm = 8.8mm - 9mm for safety

Fig 4 Router cutters used and housing produced with them

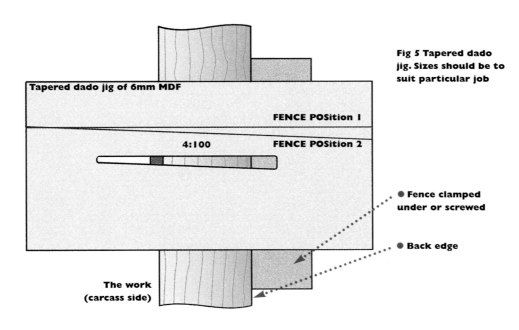

Tapered dado jig of 6mm MDF

FENCE POSition I

4:100   FENCE POSition 2

Fig 5 Tapered dado jig. Sizes should be to suit particular job

● Fence clamped under or screwed

● Back edge

The work (carcass side)

ABOVE: Photo 3 Routing the housing

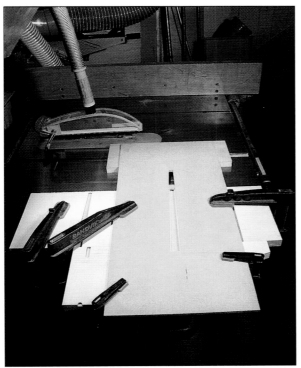

ABOVE: Photo I Dado jig clamped in place

BELOW: Photo 2 Relationship between the cut housing and dado jig

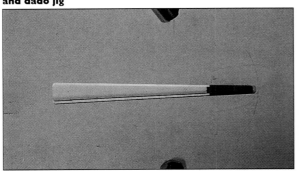

Dado jig

The dado jig is made from 6mm MDF, *see photos 1 and 2,* in which the relationship between the jig and the housing cut can also be seen.

The tapered opening in the jig is made by repositioning a straight fence after making the first — square — cut, the router being simply guided by its straight edge, *see fig 5.* The fence on the jig is held with two small clamps as the fence must be positioned on the opposite surface for routing the housings in the opposite side of the carcass.

These components are as usual mirror images of each other. With 14mm guide bushes installed both router cutters are set to cut at the correct depth, 5.2mm.

There must be a little clearance at the base of the housing so that the shoulder is not held open and the dovetail surface makes a tight fit, *see fig 6.* Several housings were routed in scrap for the gluing test, *see photo 3.*

Horizontal router

A horizontal router set up on the sawbench, *see photo 4,* is ideal for routing the dovetailed shoulder on the shelves. I would not fancy machining wide shelves vertically over a conventional router table.

With the blade and fence removed, the Wadkin 10in AGS sawbench provides a larger surface on which the shelves can be supported horizontally. An 8mm hole drilled in the machine edge of the left-hand side provides a fixing for the apparatus.

A fence made from a length of 12mm MDF with a matching hole for 8mm studding and an opening through which the cutter will protrude is clamped to the sawbench edge at either end, *see photo 5.*

The top of the router table — from the ELU router accessory kit — is attached with the same length of studding, and the ELU MOF96 is in situ on its bars with the fine lateral and depth adjusters installed.

To raise the cutter to its approximate working height, the router assembly is pivoted about the studding and fixed with a 150mm quick-acting clamp to the edge, from underneath, *see photo 6.*

Tapered support

The shelves have to sit on a tapered support while the 'rebate' is machined in the end-grain. This consists of a 6mm rectangle of MDF with wedges of the correct slope glued on underneath, *see fig 7.*

A stop is screwed to the top surface to ensure that all shelves

Fig 6

● Gap to allow for shoulder to be pulled up

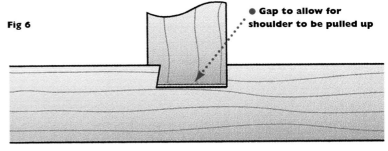

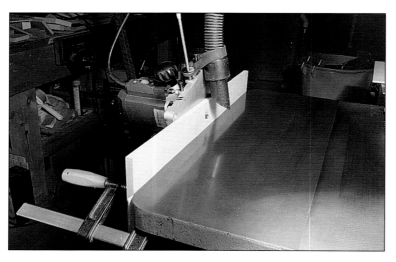

TOP LEFT: **Photo 4** Set-up viewed from table side, showing fence and cutter

BELOW LEFT: **Photo 5** The fence is fixed with quick-acting clamps

TOP RIGHT: **Photo 6** Horizontal router set-up showing studding used for fixing and quick-acting clamp

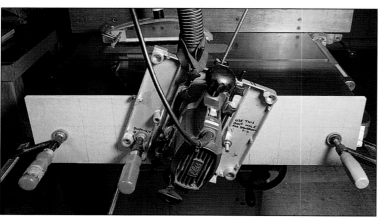

RIGHT: Fig 7 Tapered support used to rout ends of shelves; the cut is parallel to sawbench table

Fig 8 Simple taper jig to produce wedges for shelf support jig

Bandsaw blade ●

Next wedge cut off with stock against ● fence (readjust)

Saw kerf 1 ●

Saw kerf 2 ●

Wedge cut off here ●

18mm MDF

taper jig 6mm MDF

Fence

Stop glued on ●

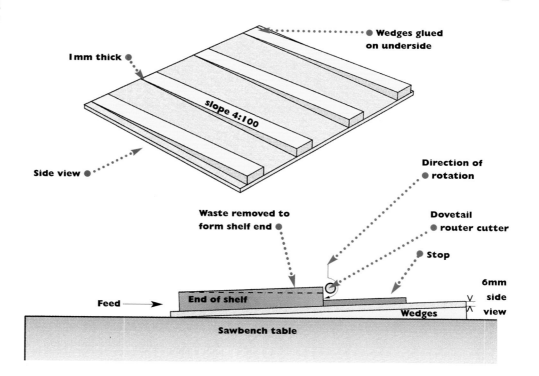

● Wedges glued on underside

1mm thick ●

slope 4:100

Side view ●

Waste removed to form shelf end ●

Direction of ● rotation

Dovetail ● router cutter

● Stop

Feed ➞

End of shelf

Wedges

6mm side view

Sawbench table

sit in the same place on the slope.

The work is passed under the dovetail router cutter rather than over, so dealing with slight variations of thickness if several shelves are to be machined. The wedges are produced with a simple taper jig used on the bandsaw, *see fig 8*.

Before cutting the wedges, I checked that the slope was correct by cutting a test wedge rather thicker and offering it up to the guide slot in the dado jig.

Small adjustments

This test revealed that a small adjustment to the taper jig was required. When the wedges had been cut slightly over-length they were not all identical in thickness, so the thin ends were offered up to a thin parallel space and a pencil line drawn at the point where they stuck.

This line acted as a reference point when they were glued to the 6mm MDF.

'Creeping up' on the finished dimensions with the aid of the fine adjusters means plenty of test pieces must be made.

> "The work is passed under the dovetail router cutter rather than over, so dealing with slight variations of thickness if several shelves are to be machined"

■ **Because of the danger of cumulative errors creeping in during the description and execution of this precise joint, metric measurements have not been converted into imperial.**

The height adjustment is a little awkward because of the massive backlash in the mechanism, so it helps to apply hand pressure to be sure that the router is really descending when the knurled wheel is turned. The other solution to backlash is to lower much too far and then climb back up to position, *see panel*.

A deep knife or chisel cut close to the final cut line reduces the problem of furry edges from the routing, and is much easier to achieve than a cut exactly in the right place.

Results

My attempt to describe this process has been far more difficult than the example was to produce. The results from these simple jigs were a beautiful fit and seemed to be reliably repeatable. I can only conclude that if there are many of these joints to produce the effort is well worthwhile; however, if only a few are required the hand tool method wins hands down, *see photo 10.* ■

BELOW RIGHT:
Photo 10 Finished joint

ALL IN THE ANGLE?

Simon Clark, a friend and an excellent cabinetmaker with a no-compromise attitude, is currently working on an 18-seat dining table with three solid timber pedestals which employ a tapered dovetail housing where the legs join the pillar.

His 1:60 taper is much flatter than the example shown here, and all his test joints stopped 8 to 10mm short when glued with PVA. All his joints were carefully cut with substantial jigs but there was still a slight variation in his results.

Returning to the example shown, I was confidently expecting it to stop short when the glue was applied. However, when steady force was supplied from a long, quick-acting clamp I was dumbfounded to find that this was not the case, see photos 7 & 9. Whether this was something to do with my choice of veneered MDF or the rather steep taper angle remains to be discovered.

ABOVE: **Photo 7 Closing joint with quick-acting clamp and pressure blocks to protect the work**

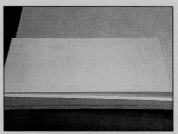

ABOVE: **Photo 9 Finishing shelf rebate showing the tapered support**

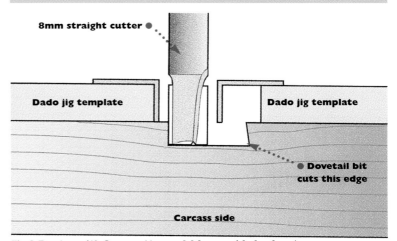

8mm straight cutter ●

Dado jig template

Dado jig template

● **Dovetail bit cuts this edge**

Carcass side

Fig 9 Router with 8mm cutter and 14mm guide bush cuts approximately 3mm smaller than template

TELLING THE TIME

I USE an indicator taped to the wheel on my router to visualise how many 'minutes on the clock' it has moved, *see photo 8.*

The pitch of this 8mm metric thread is one millimetre, so six 'minutes on the clock' amount to 0.1mm adjustment. The fine depth adjuster has a 6mm metric thread whose pitch is not quite so convenient, but five minutes on the clock is slightly less than 0.1mm.

I try to calibrate all my machines in this fashion, noting the results by the handwheels in felt tip. An arrow to indicate the direction of rotation for up or down can also save mistakes.

LEFT: **Photo 8 Machining the dovetail rebate in a shelf; note the vertical adjuster with the yellow sticker and indicator**

ABOVE: A thing of beauty is a joy forever. Photo by Ron Lucking

A joy forever

On the rightness of design,
dowelling and quality hardware

THIS WALL cupboard, designed with my fourth student, John Elbert, in 1982, is one of my favourite pieces. It is one of those rare designs which seem to be almost perfect; despite careful scrutiny over a 15 year period, I would be tempted to change almost nothing if we needed to make another today.

That is not something I could say about its companion piece, a sideboard, which stands below it. Although this was beautifully made in a similar style, it lacks 'rightness'. We perceived this even before it was finished, but no matter how hard we tried to play with the design elements it would not 'sing'.

This phenomenon has recurred over the years, and I have also noticed it in exhibition work and in the wide variety of designs which we study in books and magazines. The number of pieces which really work and have that feeling of tranquillity, beauty and rightness are few.

James Krenov

The work of James Krenov was an overwhelming influence on this cupboard made from olive ash, *see panel*.

The construction of the carcass is dowelled, with a frame and panel back. The doors are hung on knife hinges and the arrangement of stiles and rails in the glazed doors was given a lot of consideration.

The width of each element is different from its neighbour. The top and bottom rails run uninterrupted through the centre, which is set back by 1.5mm (¹⁄₁₆in) to further emphasise this effect.

Grain selection played an important part too. The top and bottom rails have gently arched, symmetrical curves

BELOW: Hand-ground lip and spur bits

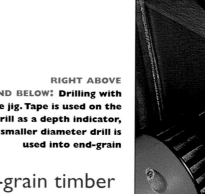

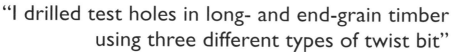

"I drilled test holes in long- and end-grain timber using three different types of twist bit"

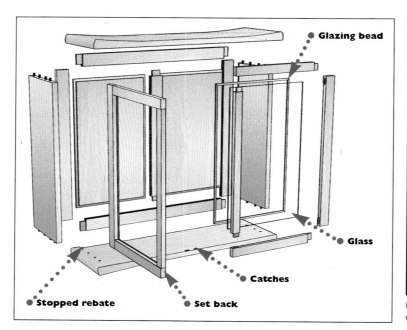

● Glazing bead

● Glass

● Catches

● Stopped rebate   ● Set back

TIMBER CHOICE

FINDING SUITABLE timber is always a problem. Photographer, Windsor chair maker and close friend Bob Seymour discovered a timber yard near Honiton owned by an enthusiast called John Toy, who had some wide boards of magnificently figured 1½in olive ash stashed away.

Machining revealed a pleasing ripple effect – which provided a dilemma as another purchase of 1in stuff for the doors and panels was mainly white.

In my opinion highly figured timber is not suitable for narrow door elements, and centre-deeping thick timber is an invitation for all kinds of cupping and bowing.

An experiment bleaching a scrap of the olive ash with powerful two-pack bleach obtainable from polish suppliers was successful, and the olive ash was transformed to an ivory which sits comfortably with the plain ash.

These chemicals are highly caustic so great care and thick rubber gloves are required.

running through their length, the balance of these curves being carefully arranged to tie in with the sweep of the top and bottom edge of the carcass.

The stiles were selected with straight grain to harmonise with the vertical sides. The widths of the rails and stiles were established by drawing and trial and error.

Making the bottom rail wider than the top rail helps to put visual weight at the base of the door.

The hinging stiles covering the carcass edge are relatively wide to balance the combined visual weight of rails and carcass which 'add together' in the horizontal.

DON'T SKIMP ON DETAILS

FINDING APPROPRIATE hinges for small cabinets and boxes is a major preoccupation of mine. While good quality solid drawn brass butts are to be had – avoid bubble-packed varieties and dress up with a file – small-scale special purpose brassware does not seem to be available in this country.

Compare the scale and finish of the hinges illustrated. The nylon washer is an abomination and the pin was a sloppy fit in its hole even before use, whereas the beautiful, accurately machined straight knife hinge is part of a 'cabinet jewellery' range – some of which also comes in German silver – made by Larry and Faye Brusso, available mail order from The Japan Woodworker in California, tel 0015 1052 11810, fax 0015 1052 11864. Fairly expensive, they are worth every cent.

The hinge problem also applies to door catches and stops. The Krenov-type door catch, pictured, from another job, may also be made with an integral door stop, *see fig 3*. They close with a pleasing woody click, and doors may be opened without having to put a foot on the wall.

There's no need to cannibalise Biros, a modelling shop will sell a lifetime's supply of small springs for about a pound.

Another subtle detail is a small raised, inlaid pad to stop the doors grinding away the finish on the base of the carcass if the weight of the glass makes the doors droop a bit. This may be incorporated with a door stop, *see fig 3*.

Small pieces of exotic hardwood are best for these and also for handles and knobs, but for very PC makers hornbeam, box or plum would be suitable.

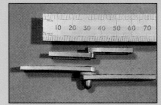

ABOVE RIGHT & LEFT: Brusso and English knife hinges

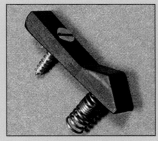

RIGHT: Krenov-type door catch

ABOVE & RIGHT: Brusso box stop hinges

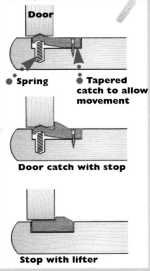

Door

● **Spring** ● **Tapered catch to allow movement**

Door catch with stop

Stop with lifter

Fig 3 Door catch mechanisms

"Tapping a glued dowel to its correct depth only to see it rise up again on a pneumatic cushion of air is disconcerting"

The closing stiles are made as narrow as is structurally feasible so that their combined weight does not overwhelm the centre.

After all, a display cabinet should not have heavy bars obstructing the view.

Shaping

Shaping the top and bottom of the carcass involved removing a great deal of thickness from one side of the boards. This is very similar to the centre deeping, *see Timber Choice panel*, which I have just advised strongly against!

We quickly accomplished the rough shaping and left the timber to settle for as long as possible, with plenty of allowance for correcting movement later. These boards had been air-dried for many years and there was much

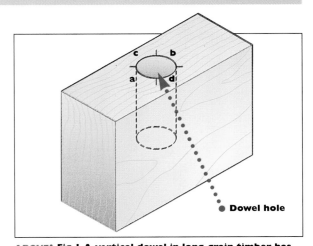

ABOVE: Fig 1 A vertical dowel in long-grain timber has reduced glue strength due to the large area of end-grain in the drilled hole. Quadrants A and B are almost entirely end-grain, with poor glue strength. Quadrants C and D are the only areas with good glue strength

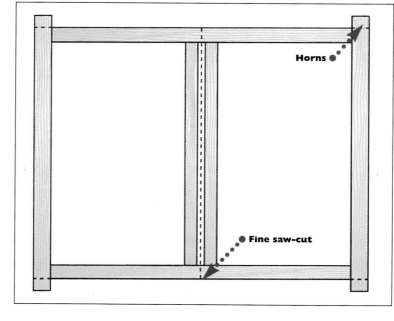

less movement than we expected.

The majority of the waste was removed with varying depth cuts on the crosscut saw. The final shaping of the curved surface was achieved with a variety of tools and a lot of patience. The elliptical curves at either end were finished with a compass plane while the flat centre was perfected with a number $10^{1}/_{2}$ rebate plane used diagonally wherever possible.

I have always found the compass plane rather difficult to use where the curve is not a true radius. The trick seems to be to set the sole radius slightly tighter than the work for internal curves and a trifle flatter for convex ones, balancing the mouth area on the work. I would welcome comments from regular users.

The surfaces were perfected with a scraper and shaped sanding blocks.

Carcass construction

This particular piece was dowelled together using the classic Krenov method. Tapered dovetail housings, through wedged tenons with housings, and biscuits have all been used on subsequent pieces.

I am not a great fan of dowelled joints for other purposes as the useful gluing area of a dowel fitted across the grain – as they usually are – is not great, *see fig 1*.

Because precisely sized holes in the correct place are extremely difficult to achieve in the wood workshop, I drilled test holes in long and end-grain timber using three different types of twist bit: a standard engineer's bit, a home-produced lip and spur bit and a commercial lip and spur bit.

In all cases the end grain hole and long grain hole were of differing diameter, slightly over 0.1mm – an over-tight dowel might easily split the carcass side when it has swelled up with the application of water-based glue.

Krenov's solution is to grind lip and spur bits from high quality HSS (high speed steel) engineer's bits like Dormer's. Data tables provide sizes, and it should be possible to find two bits, slightly different in diameter, with which to produce a nice fit in both halves of the carcass joint.

The regrinding of the tip is made easier if done slowly with a simple angled rest. A felt-tip guide line may be added to aid symmetry when a suitable shape has been achieved on one side.

The tip may be checked for error by running the bit in drill press or lathe. Reground bits cut very clean holes and are much less prone to wandering at the start of the hole.

Dowel quest

Finding good quality dowels may also pose problems, the widely available ramin lengths being neither round nor accurately sized.

Some form of fluting, whether spiral or straight, is essential. Gluing is assisted and the dreaded piston effect is avoided, as air and excess glue are provided with an escape route. Tapping a glued dowel to its correct depth only to see it rise up again on a pneumatic cushion of air is disconcerting.

High quality commercially made dowel is available; if a small quantity cannot be scrounged from a local manufacturer, ramin may be driven through a suitably undersized hole drilled in a bought or home-made steel plate. Better still, plane up or cleave some octagons of straight-grained hardwood.

Several famous workshops use threaded rod (studding) with West Epoxy and suitable fillers in place of tenons or wooden dowels.

Horns ●

● Fine saw-cut

> "An experiment bleaching a scrap of the olive ash with powerful two-pack bleach obtainable from polish suppliers was successful"

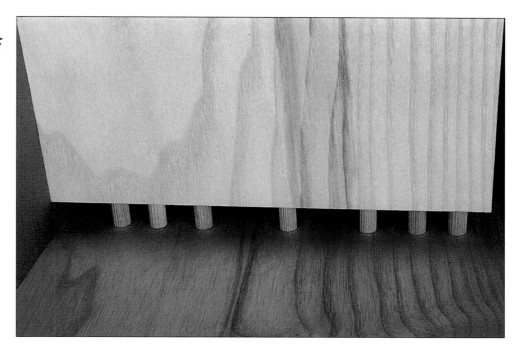

RIGHT: The completed joint

The beauty of the Krenov method is that a workshop-made dowelling jig, produced from a scrap of hardwood, is tailored to the job. My example uses 8mm ($^5/_{16}$in) dowels spaced at approximately one per 25mm (1in), but it may be beneficial to have the dowels more closely spaced towards the edges as these are the potential joint failure spots. Remember the rebate for the back – wiping out two-thirds of a dowel when this is machined is irritating. A 4mm ($^5/_{32}$in) dowel could provide support to the thin edge where the rebate has been cut.

The jig
When the squareness of the table has been checked and adjusted – important as the jig will be used upside down for some drilling – the holes are drilled in a pillar drill, against a simple fence.

The timber should be accurately thicknessed with a good face edge which is always orientated to the inside of the carcass and aligned with the inner face of the sides.

A simple end stop is screwed to the back end of the jig so that it may register on the back edge of the carcass elements.

Two small holes are also provided so that slender hardened nails, such as those used for picture hanging, may be tapped a short way into the work to stop the jig from slipping in use.

When drilling the holes, pay attention to squareness and use some kind of depth stop or marker. The holes in the carcass top and base should stop 5mm ($^3/_{16}$in) away from the finished outer surface to prevent ghosting through when the glue shrinks and dries. If using two slightly different sized drills, utilise the smaller for the jig and drill all the corresponding holes first.

Or use the router method, *see panel.*

One last precaution. When the dowels are glued into the carcass sides before final assembly, *see photo,* their protrusion should be carefully checked against a simple block.

Knife hinges
That mention of gluing up was premature. The knife hinges used are practically impossible to fit after gluing up so the doors should be made first.

All door hanging, fitting and checking of catches and stops, checking that the closing stiles line up, plus internal finishing, should be completed before the carcass glue up.

Glue up both doors as one unit, sawing apart the top and bottom rails when dry, *see fig 2.* ■

PERSPEX TEMPLATE TRICK

A CUNNING router method has been devised by my talented friends Terry Sawle and Malcolm Vaughan from Littleham Workshop. A 6mm ($^{15}/_{64}$in) Perspex template is drilled with a sawtooth bit so that the holes exactly fit a guide bush on the base of an Elu MOF 96E router.

In the example, *see picture,* 14mm ($^{35}/_{64}$in) diameter was selected. This template is attached to the work with countersunk head screws and the holes drilled by plunging with an 8 or 10mm ($^5/_{16}$ or $^3/_8$in) TCT router drill bit – available from Trend

ABOVE: A device for removing recalcitrant dowels

– set on the slowest speed.

The beauty of this system is that the jig does not wear out and that the holes are more uniform in diameter. Their metal plate has two sizes of hole, one for checking the final assembly dowels and one

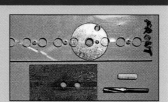

ABOVE: Steel plate for sizing dowels, router drill bit, Perspex dowelling jig with router guide bush and commercial dowel

to produce slightly undersized dowels for dry glue ups.

Removal of tight dowels can be difficult, but the simple device illustrated is invaluable, doing little damage to the dowel.

Seat of cor

Making a meditation stool in yew

Ergonomic seating

UNLESS YOU HAVE an interest in meditation, you are unlikely to be familiar with this type of seat which is often mistaken for an African or Chinese pillow, but is in fact a kneeling stool, *see photo 2.*

I came across the concept some years ago while doing insight meditation at Gaia House in South Devon. The traditional posture for Buddhist meditation is the Lotus position, but this is not always possible for the un-supple Western frame.

The practice consists of sitting still for 45 minutes while attempting to clear the mind of the barrage of random thoughts which usually assail it. This is a long time to remain still, and if the head and upper body are not stress-free and relaxed, the muscles start to complain.

The stool takes stress away from the knees, the spine is balanced on the sitting bones, and the head can sit comfortably on top of the spine.

This is precisely the kind of posture that modern ergonomic

seating such as the Balans range is designed to achieve, and is surprisingly comfortable for activities such as watching television. I like to use mine when my back is playing up – I suspect that bad backs are endemic in the furniture making world!

ABOVE: Photo 3 The maquette – essential aid in designing any kind of seating

"The stool takes stress away from the knees, the spine is balanced on the sitting bones, and the head can sit comfortably on top of the spine"

Experiment

If you intend to make one of these stools I would suggest a simple mock up, as you will need to change the height and slope of the seat for individual fit – this will vary from person to person due to flexibility of the feet and ankles.

BELOW: Graceful and ergonomic – kneeling stool in yew

emplation

A. C. LITTLEJOHNS

You may need to re-position the stabilizing foot – I have seen the stool made with no foot at all, but that might be a bit extreme for everyday use.

Design

I started work on the stool with my student, Güstav Lunning, and once we had sorted out the basic parameters we did some sketching – the outline shape and concept were soon established.

He produced the maquette, *see photo 3*, which helped us to visualize the finished object.

The plan was to use a housed joint, with through-wedged tenons, mitred at the front and back. This mitred detail is often found in antique Chinese furniture – the main advantage being that symmetrical mouldings flow uninterrupted round drawer openings and dividers, and even down the edges of legs, *see photo 4*.

In England, this detail would usually have to be achieved with a mason's mitre or an applied moulding. The best known modern example is found in the low benches made by Alan Peters.

Drawing

For the drawing stage, Güstav retired to his comfortable digs and large drawing board for a couple of afternoons, and came back with a superb working drawing, *see fig 1*. He had sorted out all the details and precise shapes which contribute to the beauty of this elegant design.

Timber

He was keen to experiment with some English yew (*taxus baccata*) as he had not worked with anything of this nature during his two years at the Karl Malmsten school in Stockholm.

I happened to have a whole butt of yew stored in the roof, which a friend had found for me many years ago. It was not particularly good and we had to turn over the whole stack to find one plank with enough clear timber to do this relatively small job – which was a good example of the 300% waste figure which is often quoted for difficult English timbers like walnut (*juglans regia*) and yew.

The joint

It became apparent that there are many different possibilities for the main joint. The classic shelf joint for wide carcasses is shown in Bob Wearing's *The Essential Woodworker* (Batsford, ISBN 0 7134 8005 X) – but our example is not wide, so the housing could be dispensed with altogether, and this would make it a much simpler job!

I don't really like plain or bare-faced housings as it is all too easy to bruise and chip the corners, which would detract from the crispness of the fit – hence the decision to have two small shoulders.

You will notice that in Güstav's drawing the housing has been taken about half way through the thickness of the top, and I think this has probably contributed to the slight opening of one face of the front mitre.

ABOVE LEFT: Photo 4 A large stool in walnut which was made for a client in 1977. They had a beautiful Chinese sideboard from which the joinery details were largely taken

ABOVE: Photo 2 Bob Seymour shows the benefits for the back of this simple concept

"For the drawing stage, Güstav retired to his comfortable digs and large drawing board for a couple of afternoons, and came back with a superb drawing"

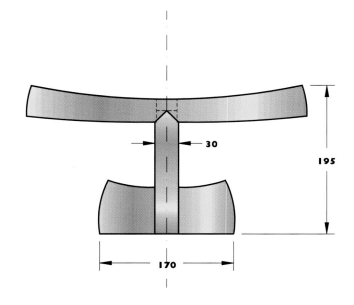

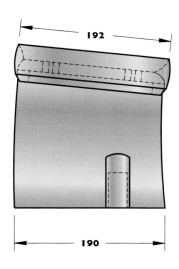

30

195

170

192

190

Fig 1

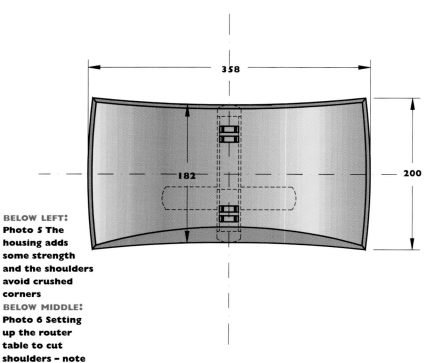

358

182

200

"The main problem is the tilt of the seat, so we kept enough extra width at the front edge of the vertical support, and marked everything out from the back edge"

My example, *see photo 5*, has a much more modest housing which is quite sufficient and probably gives some extra strength – another possibility which comes to mind is shown in fig 2.

Marking and Cutting

The joint is only really possible from a face side and edge, so it is essential to keep the wood square until the cutting and fitting are completed.

The main problem is the tilt of the seat, so we kept enough extra width at the front edge of the vertical support, and marked everything out from the back edge. Many marking-gauge settings were required!

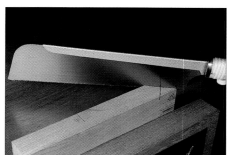

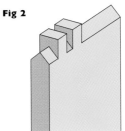
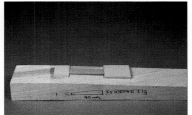

Construction

We decided to cut the through mortices first on the usual principle that it is easier to adjust tenons than mortices.

All the faces are pared or chopped to final size as our morticer tends to massacre end grain and would not have left a clean finish on the show side. It is important to ensure that the long sides of the mortices are flat, as there is quite a lot of thickness to be removed from the top surface, in the shaping of the seat.

Check the entry and exit widths carefully – a fit is impossible if the exit is wider than the entry.

The stopped housing is routed next – to full depth, with a certain amount of space for excess glue – keeping slightly away from the shoulder lines, which are chopped with a wide chisel.

Tenon widths may now be marked through the mortices and sawn by hand, bandsaw, or circular saw. As usual I find it preferable to make these cuts on the bandsaw where I am confident of producing a result to within 0.1mm.

It is difficult to define tolerances as there are different requirements for different species. My example is in Dutch elm (*ulmus hollandica*) which is easily compressible, while the original stool is in yew, which is quite hard and brittle and could be split with an over-tight joint.

Checking is assisted by the use of plastic dial calipers – Rabone Chesterman, RAB699 metric or RAB700 imperial from APTC catalogue, *see suppliers, next page.*

Routing

Before routing the shoulders on the tenon piece, and fitting to the housing, fill the saw-cuts with pine so that the corners of the tenons will be less likely to be chipped off, *see photo 6.*

Again, both cuts will have to be stopped to avoid cutting a step into the mitred section. I like to set a stop deliberately short and then move it by the amount of miss on the first cut.

This is a much less worrying operation than trying to determine where the edge of the cutter is, particularly on table operations where the cutter is often hidden by the work.

Final marking and paring

As before, shoulder lines are chopped with a wide chisel and then the line for the depth of housing re-gauged from the end, so that the waste can be sawn and cut away.

After checking the fit, the mitres are roughly sawn in, *see photo 7,* and the joint entered.

I like to leave the final marking of the seat-mitre to this stage as variations in the tenons could have displaced the leg off-centre. APTC now sell a useful engineer's mitre-square which is available in two sizes, WEZ 2404 100mm, or WEZ 2406 150mm, *see suppliers, next page.*

All final paring of mitres is done with the aid of the mitre-guide, *see photo 8.*

These joints are difficult to perfect as a small error in cutting or marking seems to translate into an unreasonably large gap, *see photo 9.*

Jig

A jig is used to make the tiny wedges on the bandsaw, *see photos 5 and 10.* We have tried most of the other methods over the years and I am convinced that this is the most effective.

Each wedge is identical and the jig is easy to make. It is used against a straight fence on the bandsaw and the previously thicknessed timber is flipped top to bottom after each cut. The blade must give a good finish and it may be necessary to fix a false table so that the wedges do not fall down the throat.

Bridle joint

The bridle joint for the foot is fairly straightforward, although I find it quite tricky to get a really good fit.

My current approach is to fractionally taper the sides of the housed section and plane the mating part. The tapering may be as little as a scrap of paper introduced under the stock of a square to tilt it a fraction.

ABOVE FAR LEFT:
Photo 8 Mitre guide being used to pare mitre

ABOVE LEFT:
Photo 10 Wedge-making jig

ABOVE: Photo 9 Finished halves of joint

Fig 2

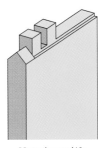
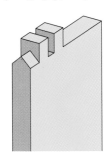

Mitred all the way through

Housing with shoulder

No housing

A FAIR CURVE

Something that cropped up in my discussions with Güstav was the drawing of fair curves, which never seems easy at full scale.

The problem is usually not apparent at the sketching stage, particularly if the sketch is small – freehand curves look fine, and you can use French curves to tidy things up a bit.

If you are not familiar with French curves, they are plastic templates which are usually sold as a set of three in any good stationers or art shops that deal in drawing equipment.

They have a variety of edges with a range of curves – these are presumably based on ellipses, though it is possible that some may be parabolic.

Drawing

By judicious fiddling and blending together of different areas, you can draw a smooth curve of any shape. The trouble is, that they are only about ten inches long, and when you try to lay out a precise line at full size, on work or template, you run into problems.

Simon Clark has kindly put me onto a supplier of larger French curves in America and I am about to order a set, see *suppliers, below* – I would like to hear from any reader who knows of an affordable source of shipwright's curves – the kind that were once used in naval architecture.

Alternatives

We have tried several alternative methods in the workshop, such as having drawings blown up on a photocopier or tiling printouts from the CAD program on my computer. Unfortunately my software is not great at curves – but it could be the operator, of course!

The photocopy method seems to introduce distortion, and our pantograph is unreliable, so we always fall back on the time-honoured solution of bending a lath.

Our current kit, see *photo 13*, is a strip of melamine-faced hardboard set up like a child's bow.

The hardboard seems to be of uniform density and is easier than finding a perfectly straight-grained lath. The curvature is varied and lines can be blended together until a satisfactory result is obtained.

Bumps

Sighting along a line from a low angle is a good way of detecting kinks and flat spots. When a template has been prepared the slip-curve technique is also useful – a thin pencil line is drawn on white paper with the template, which is then slid sideways along the curve by a few centimeters – this will show up any bumps and hollows!

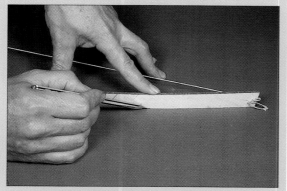

ABOVE: **Photo 13 High tech curve drawing device in use**

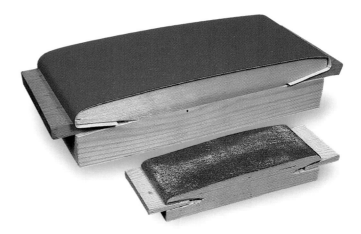

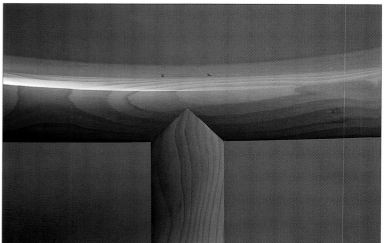

Shaping and finishing

Shaping and finishing on a job like this will call for much patience and careful work – Güstav favoured a large rasp for edge-details, followed up with a mill file. The sanding blocks which he made for the job, *see photo 11*, are quick to make and effective. A large half-round Auriou rasp is definitely on my purchasing list!

Güstav was particularly good at this, but if I hadn't seen the way he did it, I would probably have chosen spokeshaves and block planes.

When completed, apply several thinned coats of Rustins Danish oil, burnishing between coats with a 3M white pad. The oil should be diluted by about 50% with white spirit and applied sparingly.

It is vital to remove any excess within a few minutes with a dry cloth or paper towel to avoid a treacley look.

I am delighted with the finish which seems to have preserved the beauty of the yew, *see photo 12*. ■

TOP: **Photo 11 Gustav's shaped sanding blocks**

ABOVE: **Photo 12 The finished joint provides an elegant, practical detail**

> "I am delighted with the finish which seems to have preserved the beauty of the yew"

SUPPLIERS

AURIOU RASPS:
Avery Knight & Bowlers Engineering Ltd, James Street West, Bath, Avon BA1 2BT tel 01225 425894 fax 01225 445753

Axminster Power Tool Centre Chard St, Axminster Devon EX13 5DZ tel 01297 33656 fax 01297 35242

FRENCH CURVES:
Woodhaven, USA, No 3600, tel 001-800-344-6657 fax 001-319-785-6813.

"The challenge was irresistible, and after negotiating what I thought was a suitable price, I agreed to have a go"

Making inroads

The challenge of making a Japanese Inro box

SOME YEARS AGO a rather theatrically dressed lady turned up at the workshop with an intriguing box and asked if I would make her two copies.

"I've been to two other cabinetmakers and they both said they wouldn't touch it with a bargepole," she said.

This statement immediately aroused my interest, but also sounded warning bells. She told me that it was a copy of a Japanese Inro Box, and probably made in India. The timber appeared to be Indian rosewood (*Dalbergia latifolia*), and the making was somewhat crude but nonetheless effective.

The external shape is unusual but not impossible to make. The box splits into three sections which plug together rather like a woodwind instrument, but the crux of the problem lies in the shape of the interlocking parts not being circular.

For a really satisfying job the sections should plug together firmly, separating with that pleasing pneumatic pop encountered on well-made turned containers. I suspect that this was the feature that had put off my fellow cabinetmakers.

It is not difficult to achieve on a lathe, even though the tolerances involved probably amount to a mere thousandth of an inch or so, but for an object that is not circular in section… However, the challenge was irresistible, and after negotiating what I thought was a suitable price, I agreed to have a go.

Guide bush inlay

Mulling over the problem, I remembered a technique I had seen described in a magazine, in which a router with two guide bushes of different radii is employed to cut a recess, and the inlay to fit it, from one template. A straight cutter is used, its diameter being equal to the difference in radius of the two bushes.

With the larger guide bush, *see fig 1*, the cut is on one side of a line, and with the smaller bush the cut is on the other side of the same line. If the template is in the form of an aperture cut in some thin sheet material, the larger bush is used to cut the recess while the smaller bush cuts the 'inlay' to fit.

On a note of safety, the direction of feed of the router should be different for these two apparently similar operations – clockwise when viewed from above for the recess cut and anti-clockwise for the inlay cut. This ensures that the reaction force of the cutting process tends to pull the router bush into the template.

I was optimistic that this technique could be adapted to produce the interlocking parts of the box and that the same template could be used with yet another guide bush to rout the interior spaces.

Drawing

Accurate drawing is essential for this type of project, and I spent several hours working out the different radii involved. The drawings here are derived from originals that were produced on my computer, and are wonderfully neat compared to the original pencil versions.

I am still at the kindergarten stage of CAD drawing, but am hoping to become more proficient. The ability to redraw and stretch shapes is an attractive feature, while the pinpoint accuracy helps to eliminate mathematical errors.

Template

The template is made from Formica which was clamped to the vertical slide on the Myford metalworking lathe so that two

FAR LEFT: Box apart

LEFT: Box standing

"The fit was a bit sloppy and the sections fell apart rather inelegantly"

27mm, 1⁵/₆₄ in holes could be bored, a precise distance apart, with a tank cutter running at dead slow speed.

The straight sections were then machined with a milling cutter. This 'engineering' method is not absolutely necessary, but the lathe has been with me since I was 14 and I enjoy using it!

The template shown in the photograph is not my first attempt. An earlier model was made to test the guide bush technique, but the experiment was not a success. Although a reasonable fit was achieved, probably quite good enough for inlay, the pneumatic pop required for the inro box was not forthcoming.

The fit was a bit sloppy and the sections fell apart rather inelegantly. Worse still, the results did not seem to be repeatable with any consistency.

The timber of the first pair was to be kingwood (*Dalbergia cearensis*), and I was hoping to make more boxes from some African blackwood (*Dalbergia melanoxylon*) which I had bought from a musical instrument-making friend. These are both hard, dense, rosewood species.

The tolerance required for the fit was extremely critical, but –

and this is no criticism of the tool – the plunging action of the router was not rigid enough to allow me to proceed with any certainty.

Bushes

After a great deal of cursing and thought a possible solution occurred to me. If one of the bushes could be replaced by a smaller one I could turn up a series of rings to plug onto it.

Increasing the outside diameter of these rings by a thousandth of an inch at a time, it was possible to work through the series until a suitable fit was achieved, but many rings had to be produced in

order to complete the job, *see photo 1*.

They were machined on the Myford from some scrap material which I think is Tufnol. I also had to produce a new, larger template when the implications of machining the interior space had been fully worked out.

A long half inch straight bit was required, necessitating the use of the larger Elu MOF177 router. This comes with a 30mm guide bush, and I ended up making two rings for each machining operation to allow a roughing cut to be made before a lighter finishing cut.

➤

ABOVE: PHOTO 1
Guide bushes and rings, from left, 30mm bush for Elu MOF 177 with two rings to hollow box, 14mm bush for Elu MOF 96 with two rings to form recess, set of rings to form plug, with one for roughing cut

LEFT: Small ring fitted to 14mm guide bush on the Elu MOF 96 router

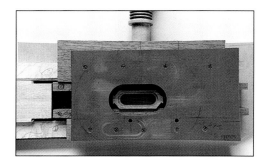

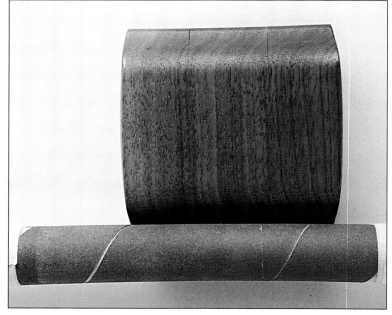

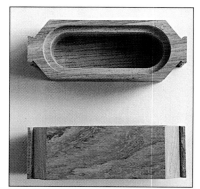

**ABOVE: Some waste is removed on
the circular saw after hollowing**

JOB FOR SOMEONE?

**THE BRITISH MUSEUM
has many Inro boxes
within its Department of
Japanese Antiquities, but,
while plenty has been
written on the subject,
no-one has yet chosen to
write about this collection
in particular.**

**Spokeswoman Sally
Morton said the
department had quite a
few on display, and that
most were in lacquer, with**
**some in ceramic or ivory.
The name 'inro' means
'seal-basket', and indicates
its origin as a small
container for the personal
carved seal and
sealing-paste which every
literate person would
carry. By the sixteenth
century it was being used
for carrying medicines or
simply for adornment,
hung from the sash by
cords.**

Remember that 'suitable price'
to which I referred earlier?

Routing out

Because the bandsaw kerf and
the 4mm, $^5/_{32}$ in plug led to about
6mm, $^1/_4$ in being lost on the
surface between each layer,
quarter-sawn timber was
selected. The jig shown, *see
photo 2*, has two wedges
protruding from the end which
hold the sections below the
template for routing. This was an
approximation of a self-centring
holding device, both wedges
being driven home together.

As exotic woods release an
unpleasant dust, and some are
toxic, extraction was attempted
by plugging a vacuum tube into
the side. The top and bottom

layers were lifted up to the same
height as the centre layer, with an
accurately made packing piece
underneath.

The deep interior routing was
done first, with a long cutter
working in small (about 5mm,
$^3/_{16}$ in) steps to full depth. Great
care was needed as there was a
lot of cutter protruding.

The roughing cuts for the plugs
and sockets were also made at
this stage, using the smaller Elu
MOF96 router. After some
settling time, the socket side was
completed.

By working up through the
series of rings until a perfect fit
was obtained, the plug side was
then machined to match its mate.

Each box was then plugged
together and clamped, so that the

outside surfaces and ends could
be trued up with a plane. The
moulded ends were then marked
out carefully on the top and
bottom with sharp engineers'
dividers, and some waste removed
on the circular saw.

The box was placed in another
simple jig and the concave
sections machined with a half inch
radius core box cutter, *see photo 3*.

Again, the box was wedged in
place to avoid tear-out between
the layers; scrap pieces were
inserted at either end for the same
reason.

The finish from this operation
was poor, so a great deal of
sanding was required; I ended up
using a home-made 'drum'
running in the lathe, *see photo 4*.
For this a long strip of wet and

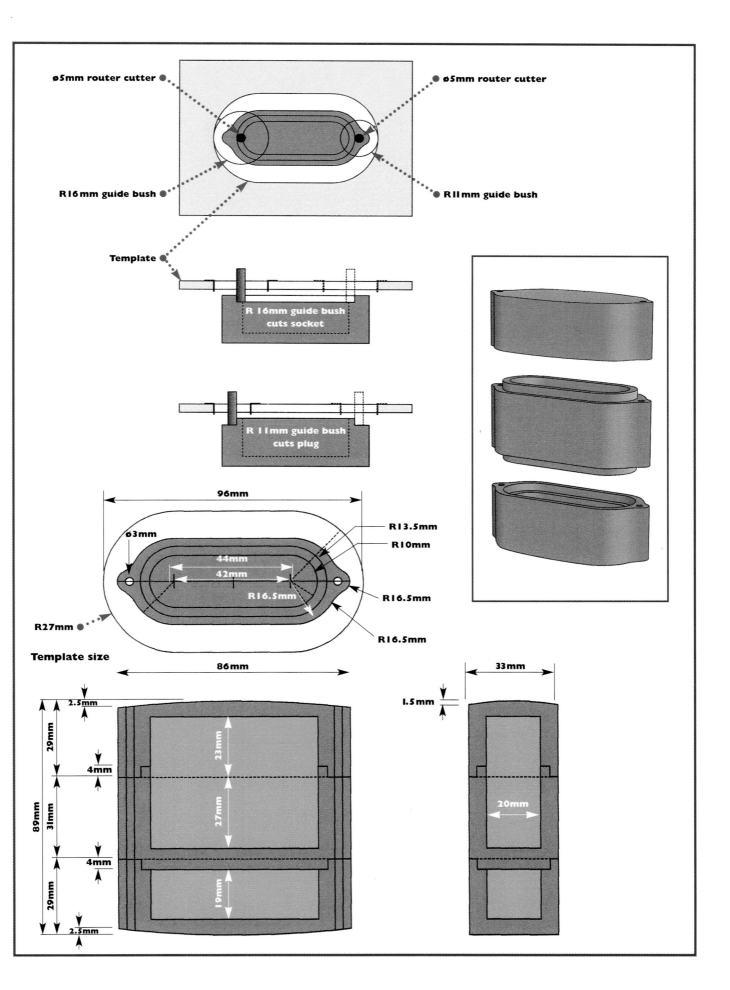

ø5mm router cutter

ø5mm router cutter

R16mm guide bush

R11mm guide bush

Template

R 16mm guide bush cuts socket

R 11mm guide bush cuts plug

96mm

ø3mm

44mm

42mm

R13.5mm

R10mm

R16.5mm

R16.5mm

R16.5mm

R27mm

Template size

86mm

33mm

2.5mm

29mm

4mm

31mm

89mm

27mm

4mm

29mm

19mm

2.5mm

23mm

1.5mm

20mm

I PARTICULARLY LIKE the shape and the beaten texture of the beads which were specially made by a jeweller friend, Charmian Harris. The silk cords were quite a performance as they had to be made by twisting three strands to form a thicker cord.

This was done with the aid of a hand drill with a coathanger hook. Each strand is given the same number of turns; when they are amalgamated the cord forms itself. The tricky task of threading this cord was made possible with the use of fuse wire, cotton and Superglue gel.

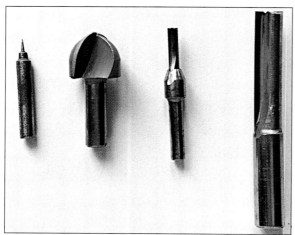

> " One of Edward Barnsley's craftsmen advised that 0000 grade wire wool can also be used on these types of wood"

TOP: PHOTO 5
Forming the convex areas with a shoulder plane

ABOVE: PHOTO 6
Cutters used and drilling pin point aid

dry abrasive paper, about an inch wide, is wound round a dowel in a spiral, secured at each end with masking tape. The direction of winding should be such that the sanding tends to tighten the spiral, not unwind it. This had the advantage of not putting cross-grain scratches into the work.

With no other method available, the convex curves were formed with a shoulder plane, care being taken not to dig the edge of the blade into the concave hollow, *see photo 5*.

Drilling aid
The holes for the silk cords were drilled with the aid of a fence and end stop for alignment. A bit of steel rod with a pin point, *see photo 6*, is very useful for setting up accurate drilling. This is especially necessary as each

section has to be drilled from both sides, so doubling any centring errors.

The curved surfaces of the top and bottom were machined on a sanding disc; the slight doming of the top was achieved with a mill file.

Sanding, finishing
Dark, close-grained woods seem to show scratches particularly badly, so the final sanding was taken down through the grades to 600 grit. The concave section is difficult, and the lathe drum proved very useful.

One of Edward Barnsley's craftsmen advised that 0000 grade wire wool can also be used on these types of wood. Another trick I remember reading, in a book by David Pye, is to use Brasso directly on the wood;

however, this can leave a pale deposit in the grain – this tip worked well on the kingwood but not so well on the blackwood.

Recently I discovered that Liberon burnishing cream will also produce a stunning sheen on rosewood. My winding sticks (*see How to unwind, page 44*) were finished like this. However, it is always wise to experiment on some scrap before making a decision.

Estimate exceeded
Commercially sensitive readers will have worked out from the above that my original estimate was greatly exceeded in both time and effort. Still, the project gave me enormous satisfaction, and people who handle the boxes are intrigued and fascinated.

I'll know how much to charge next time!

Making a wooo

How to give a modern edge to a traditional tool

I WAS BROWSING through Ron Hock's website recently when I came across one of their new lines – blades for wooden spokeshaves, and, being curious, I ordered a pair, *see photo 1*.

At about the same time I lent Dirk Lange, a student of mine from Germany, some of my spokeshaves and he was particularly enthusiastic about an old wooden one which I had bought from a second hand tool shop, *see photo 2*.

It's difficult to find old wooden spokeshaves with blades that are not badly rust-pitted or worn away, so I started thinking about making one with one of the new Hock blades which are thick, carbon steel, hardened to Rockwell 62, and hold a sharp edge.

Adjustment mechanism

The blade on my spokeshave differs from the traditional type, *see photo 1*, in that the forged tapered square tangs are replaced by two lengths of threaded studding and the blade is fixed to the body with two brass knurled nuts. The blade rests on the heads of two countersunk, sheet metal screws, *see photo 3* – fine control of shaving thickness is achieved by adjusting these screws, to raise or lower the blade, *see fig 1*.

> "I should warn you that blade preparation takes quite a lot of time and effort!"

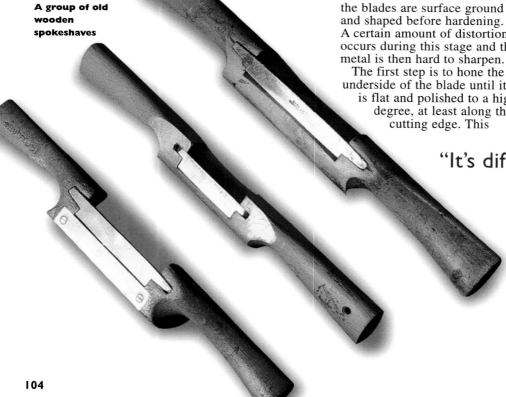

ABOVE: Photo 1
A Hock spokeshave blade with brass knurled fixing nuts

BELOW: Photo 2
A group of old wooden spokeshaves

Blade preparation

I should warn you that blade preparation takes quite a lot of time and effort! This is because the blades are surface ground and shaped before hardening. A certain amount of distortion occurs during this stage and the metal is then hard to sharpen.

The first step is to hone the underside of the blade until it is flat and polished to a high degree, at least along the cutting edge. This could be done on any sharpening medium but I use Japanese waterstones and work through grades 800 grit to 1200 grit, finishing on 6000 or 8000 grit.

At each stage, the objective is to polish out all traces of the previous underlying scratches. The first step will take the longest as the original surface grinding marks are quite deep. The blade must be held flat on the stone, so holding by the

> "It's difficult to find old wooden spokeshaves with blades that are not badly rust-pitted or worn away, so I started thinking about making one"

en spokeshave

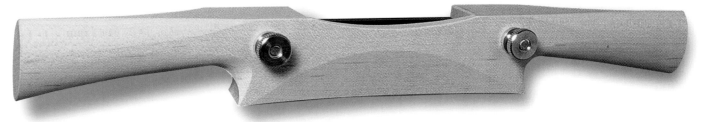

"When I looked at some of the old blades in the workshop, I noticed that the flat side is in fact slightly hollow in its width, which is perhaps the result of manufacturers grinding on a large sandstone wheel"

studding is probably not a good idea, as it would be easy to start rocking it. Waterstones are soft, so it's best to flatten and check about every five minutes.

I lap the stones on 240 grit wet and dry which is stuck to a piece of float glass by surface tension. If pencil lines are drawn all over the surface of the stone they will disappear when the stone is flat.

When I looked at some of the old blades in the workshop, I noticed that the flat side is in fact slightly hollow in its width, which is perhaps the result of manufacturers grinding on a large

sandstone wheel. This made me wonder if I could get the same effect on the Tormek, the advantage being that flat side polishing would be much quicker as you would be flattening a much smaller area of metal.

I made a simple Perspex jig, *see photo 4* – the results, *see photo 5*, are not as tidy as I would have liked, as my Tormek wheel has worn down to about 8in in diameter. This meant that I had to take several passes while hollowing, rather than one single one. But the result was quite adequate and it took less time than it might have done.

Bevel sharpening
Bevel sharpening is another awkward operation. Ron Hock's excellent instructions outlined a method which has been discussed a lot on the Internet, known as 'scary sharp', which is simply a substitution of wet and dry for sharpening stones.

BELOW LEFT: **Photo 3 Adjustment screws fitted**

BELOW: **Photo 4 Perspex jig on Tormek to hollow blade back**

"At each stage, the objective is to polish out all traces of the previous underlying scratches"

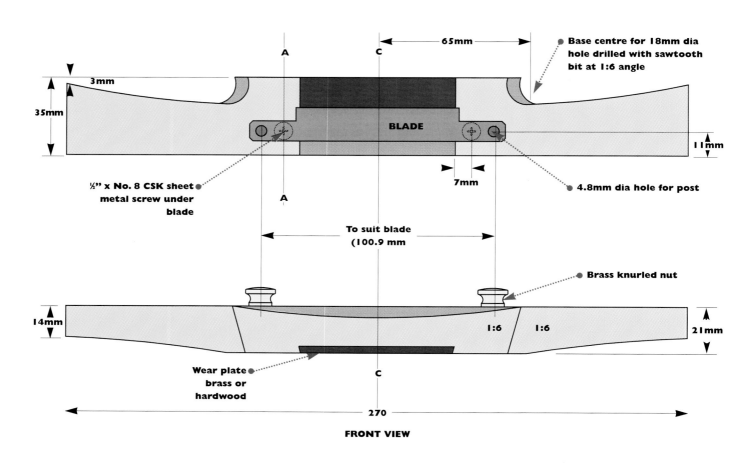

65mm

Base centre for 18mm dia hole drilled with sawtooth bit at 1:6 angle

3mm

35mm

BLADE

11mm

½" x No. 8 CSK sheet metal screw under blade

7mm

4.8mm dia hole for post

To suit blade (100.9 mm

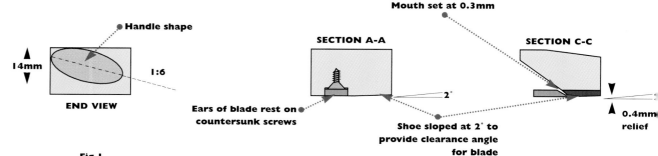

Brass knurled nut

14mm

1:6   1:6

21mm

Wear plate brass or hardwood

C

270

FRONT VIEW

Mouth set at 0.3mm

Handle shape

14mm

1:6

SECTION A-A

SECTION C-C

END VIEW

Ears of blade rest on countersunk screws

Shoe sloped at 2° to provide clearance angle for blade

2°

0.4mm relief

Fig 1

Grades as fine as 2000 grit are widely available and 3M produce diamond paper down to half a micron! I chose to use my waterstones as usual and found that the blade could be held in a jig, *see photo 6.*

Timber selection

I found a good piece of African Ebony (*Diospyros spp*) on which I installed a 2.5mm brass wear-plate – I got the brass from a model engineering supplier. Any reasonably hard, fine grained, stable hardwood should do for the stock and should be

> "A method which has been discussed a lot on the Internet, known as 'scary sharp', is simply a substitution of wet and dry for sharpening stones"

accurately planed up. The length is approximately 270 by 35 by 21mm (10⅝ by 1⅜ by ¹³⁄₁₆ in).

Being nervous of spoiling the ebony I decided to make a trial model with Canadian maple (*Acer spp*) for the body, and an inlaid ebony wear plate. In a few years time it will be interesting to see how the ebony survives.

Hole drilling

The key to success in this project is the accurately spaced hole drilling – you don't want the blade moving about in the body as this would cause chatter.

To measure the centre distance of the studding posts, measure the outside distance with calipers and subtract the diameter of one post, *see fig 3*. If a small stick is shot to exactly this length it can be used to register the two holes from a fixed stop on the drill press, *see photo 7*.

The work is kept tight against a fixed fence, which should be left in situ for later. This is a good technique, as it allows you to carry out a difficult task, using simple methods which are accurate and easy to control.

I would suggest that you drill test holes in thin scrap and then check that the blade fits, as there is very little room for error. For a close fit on the studding it is

helpful to have a set of drill bits in 0.1mm increments. I finished up drilling 4.8mm holes.

The blade is then pushed into the holes so that the position of the ears can be scribed with a scalpel, *see photo 5* .

You need a line to indicate the position of the front edge of the blade which will also define the edge of the waste, which is removed later to form the 'ware'. As I understand it, this is the sloped surface of the throat, *see fig 2*.

ABOVE: Photo 7 Drilling the post holes with stop and spacing stick

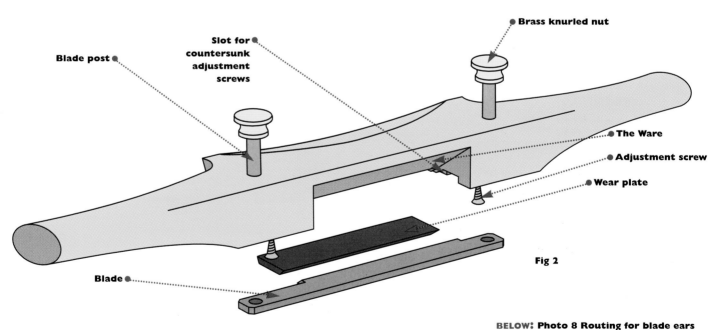

Fig 2

ABOVE: Fig 3 To find centre distance of post holes measure OD with calipers and subtract d

BELOW: Photo 8 Routing for blade ears

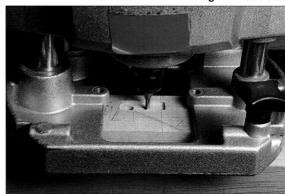

ABOVE: Photo 9 Drilling and countersinking for stainless adjusting screws

The recesses for the ears are routed in next with a 3mm diameter cutter. I did this freehand, with the other blank clamped next to the work to provide more support for the router, *see photo 8*. The depth of cut is about 0.5mm more than the thickness of the blade and there is no need to go closer to the knife lines than you dare. You can pare back the last bit with sharp chisels.

The blank can now be returned to the drill press so that the tapping holes and countersinking for the sheet metal screws, which support the blade, can be done. The sheet metal screws have nice sharp threads all the way up the shank. I used stainless ⅝in no.8 screws which had to be shortened by about 2mm. ½in might be better if you can find them. It was necessary to buy a special countersink bit, of 8.3mm diameter, to avoid messing up the sides of the recess. It seemed a good idea to start the screws in the drill press, as I wanted to avoid them going in crooked, *see photos 9 & 10*. This might have been a bit excessive, as they would probably have straightened up anyway. ■

I complete the two spokeshaves and final fettling, and test the results, in A fine pair of spokeshaves (page 110).

RIGHT: Photo 10 Driving in screws in drill press

"The key to success in this project is the accurately spaced hole drilling"

SUPPLIERS

Blades
Hock Handmade Knives, 16650 Mitchell Creek Dr. Ft. Bragg, CA 95437 tel: 001 707 964 2782 fax 001 707 964 7816 email: ron@hocktools.com

Woodcraft Supply tel: 001 800 225 1153

Traditional travishers and spokeshave irons with square posts
Bristol Designs, 14 Perry Road, Bristol, BS1 5BG tel: 0117-929-1740

A fine pair o

Completion of the two spokeshaves

IT IS NOW TIME to complete our two spokeshaves, and then for the best part – trying them out!

The Ware
The ware, which is the sloped surface of the throat, can now be marked out, sawn, and pared. It starts about 3mm (⅛in) down from the top of the back edge, *see figs 1&2*. If a wooden wear plate is to be fixed, the routing of its recess can now be done.

Ebony plate
The Ebony plate is recessed about 3mm (⅛in) and the ends are pared to a 1:6 undercut. A scrap block with this angle can be prepared as a guide. The dovetail key is probably not strictly necessary, but looks smart. It is worth noting that if the dovetail ends are used, the surface marking-out wants to be kept about 0.5mm (0.020in) or so inside the edges of the blade.

The plate is prepared slightly over thickness and the ends shot to fit, while supported on a 1:6 wooden wedge on the surface of a bench-hook shooting board. Incidentally, the ebony is prone to tear-out so all surface planing is done with a modified angle 'scraping' plane blade, *see Scraping in, page 39*.

I decided to plane the mouth edge of the plate at 45° as this would prevent the mouth opening up as the blade is sharpened. As the blade is shortened by sharpening, it can be dropped further down into the body to maintain the narrow mouth. Some material would also have to be planed off the sole and shoe of the tool.

Installing blade
The blade can now be installed and the wear plate glued in place. A piece of thin card, about 0.3mm (0.012in) was used to set the mouth opening, *see photo 1*. When the glue is dry, the plate can be planed down to the level of the sole.

> "As you can imagine, the blade will be removed and replaced many times during this project"

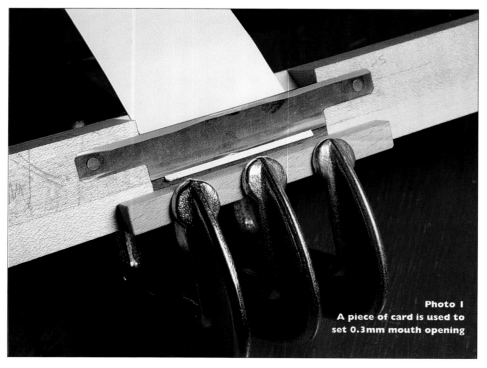

Photo I
A piece of card is used to set 0.3mm mouth opening

Photo 2 Blade-removing device in action

spokeshaves

"A correct grip is most important to get the best out of this tool"

As you can imagine, the blade will be removed and replaced many times during this project. If you use a punch to knock it out, there is a strong tendency for the blade to rack, or twist, and lock up in the holes – I therefore decided to make a blade-removing device which consists of two nails with the heads sawn off, mounted in a block. This allows both tangs to be pushed at the same time, thus avoiding racking, *see photo 2*.

The shoe
The shoe is the critical area of the sole in front of the mouth, *see fig 3*. This needs to be inclined at about 2° to the surface to give the blade some clearance angle. I tried an experiment with a chisel to confirm this – it is almost impossible to start a cut on a flat surface until the back is lifted to about this angle.

The surface is delicately planed in, a curved plane blade being of great assistance – no material should be removed from the mouth area, just adjacent to it. With my dimensions, this means gauging a line about 0.4mm (0.016in) below the front edge.

Take great care here, as this work will make or break the performance of your spokeshave.

If you want your spokeshave to work in tight concave areas, a suitable radius will need to be removed from the front edge, *see fig 3*. I decided to try a few test shavings at this stage and was pleased with the results, *see photo 3*. The pitch of my stainless screws is 1.5mm, so four minutes on the clock produces a 0.1mm blade adjustment.

"This work will make or break the performance of your spokeshave"

BELOW: **Photo 3 The acid test, trying it out on end grain – note position of hands**

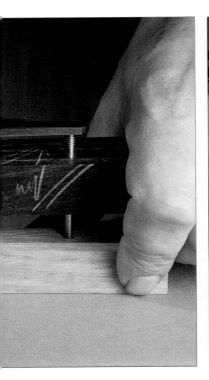

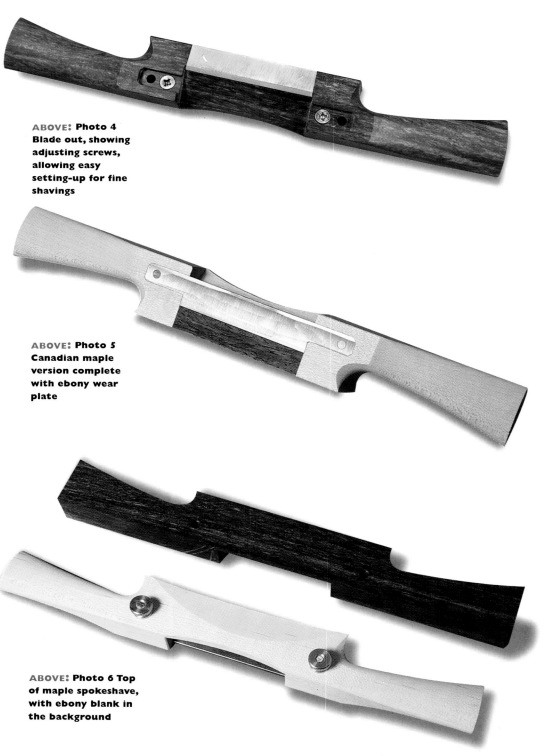

ABOVE: Photo 4 Blade out, showing adjusting screws, allowing easy setting-up for fine shavings

ABOVE: Photo 5 Canadian maple version complete with ebony wear plate

ABOVE: Photo 6 Top of maple spokeshave, with ebony blank in the background

> "Chatter is a great menace to all spokeshave work and is controlled by skewing the tool in alternate directions for successive strokes"

tightened hard, the blade seems to flex slightly along its length. This, in a small way, approximates to the curved edge which is so useful on a plane blade. Many old blades seem to have a pronounced rocker in their length.

Moving the tool laterally, relative to the work, provides control of the shaving thickness, which allows flat edges to be kept square. Another technique is to cock the blade. A tapered setting, with coarse shavings at one side and fine at the other, is useful for creating chamfers, roughing out with coarse shavings, and polishing with fine ones.

Chatter
Chatter is a great menace to all spokeshave work and is controlled by skewing the tool in alternate directions for successive strokes – and by taking finer shavings with a sharper blade! This allows the blade of the tool to bridge over and shave the tops of the bumps caused by the previous chatter. If the tool is not alternately skewed, the bumps perpetuate and increase. A good test of your tool is whether it will take fine shavings from end grain.

Blade setting
Blade setting, *see photo 4*, is fairly critical and I would suggest taking some fine shavings for practice. It may be my imagination but, if the knurled brass fixing nuts are

> "The palms can rest on top of the handles if some extra oomph is required"

TOOL MARKET

The two Harris spokeshaves with Bubinga bodies, *see photo 7*, are from The Craftsman's Choice. One is straight bladed, and designed to fit fairly tight curves. The other has a convex blade and would be useful for dished work such as chair seats – it could be used as a travisher.

Both have tough high-speed steel blades and a positive, spring loaded, screw adjustment for depth of cut. As usual, both tools will require some sharpening and tuning up for best performance.

Harris tools have an interesting catalogue of hard-to-find tools which are now being sold for the first time in this country. Axminster Power Tool Company have also included some in their new catalogue, which has a number of intriguing items.

Tool supplies seem to have improved steadily over the last twenty-five years and there has never been such a wide variety available. I feel that we are very fortunate with the current state of affairs.

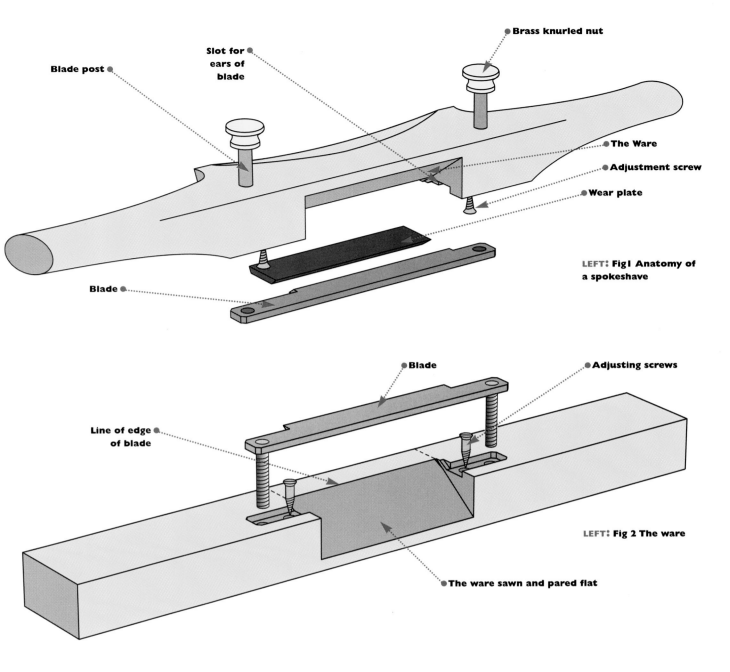

Blade post

Slot for ears of blade

Brass knurled nut

The Ware

Adjustment screw

Wear plate

LEFT: Fig 1 Anatomy of a spokeshave

Blade

Blade

Adjusting screws

Line of edge of blade

LEFT: Fig 2 The ware

The ware sawn and pared flat

"Editor, Paul Richardson, tells me that oiling the ebony wear plate regularly will help to prevent wear – an interesting tip from guitar technology!"

Maple spokeshave

My maple spokeshave, *see photos 5&6*, was photographed in the white, but the plan is to treat it with several coats of lemon oil. Editor, Paul Richardson, tells me that oiling the ebony wear plate regularly will help to prevent wear – an interesting tip from guitar technology!

I am pleased with the result and looking forward to an opportunity for some serious testing, as my initial impressions are encouraging. I find that making tools is a satisfying exercise and helps my understanding of how they work.

Ebony spokeshave

The ebony spokeshave is now finished and I am thrilled with the result! The shaping of the tool was not easy, as there are various compound curves to blend together in a pleasing manner. I did this by creating flat bevels at varying angles before refining the shape. The advantage of this method is that the width of bevel gives a good indication of the amount of material removed, which is a great help when you are trying to achieve symmetry between the two sides. Ebony takes a remarkable finish, and it was sanded through the grades to 1000 grit wet and dry.

CORRECT GRIP

A correct grip is most important to get the best out of this tool. The thumbs and second fingers grip the back and front edges as close to the blade as possible. The first fingers are used to apply pressure to the top of the shave above the shoe, see *photo 3*. The rest of the fingers are lightly supported on the handles and should not be gripping them – gripping prevents the feel and balance which are needed to maintain a shaving. The palms can rest on top of the handles if some extra oomph is required. A shaving can be stopped by rolling the tool, and climbing out of the cut. The tool can also be drawn towards you with all fingers being reversed.

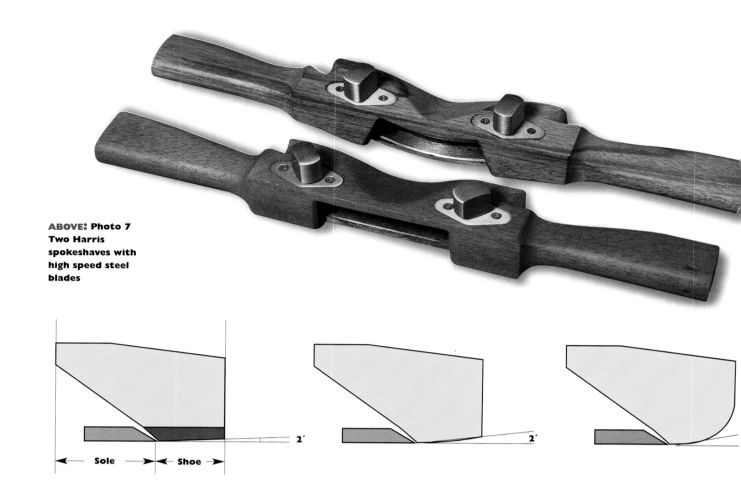

ABOVE: Photo 7 Two Harris spokeshaves with high speed steel blades

Sole → ← Shoe →

2°

2°

Differences

ABOVE: Fig 3 The shoe slopes at 2° to provide blade clearance – a suitable radius can be formed afterwards for curved work if required

There was one major difference in the method of making the ebony spokeshave – I did not want to file the brass to produce the 2° slope for the shoe. A skilled metalworker would have no problem, but I decided to plane the shoe in the ebony before routing for the brass wear plate.

The routing was done on the router table with the shoe flat on the table. Balancing the work at this angle was a little uncertain, so two shims of veneer were temporarily glued near the back edge of the sole, to improve

stability, *see fig 4*. These shims can be left attached until the brass has been fitted as they will also assist the polishing of the shoe which is now a brass and ebony composite, not suitable for planing!

The brass screws are carefully fitted, remembering to run some steel ones in first – it is all too easy to shear off a brass screw in hard woods and that would be disastrous at this stage! The countersinking was deliberately shallow so that the screw heads could be filed off flush for a neat appearance. ■

"A good test of your tool is whether it will take fine shavings from end grain"

BELOW: Fig 4 End view of routing for brass wear plate

Glue veneer shims here to keep
● 'shoe' flat on router table

Shoe ●

Sole

Router table

SUPPLIERS

Blade from **Hock Handmade Knives**, 16650 Mitchell Creek Dr. Ft. Bragg, CA 95437 tel 001 707 964 2782 fax 001 707 964 7816 email: ron@hocktools.com
Another source of supply for blades is **Woodcraft Supply** tel 001 800 225 1153
The Craftsman's Choice tel 01233 501 010 fax 01233 501 201
Axminster Power Tool Company tel 01297 33656
Bristol Design is the only supplier of traditional travishers and spokeshave irons with square posts that I know of – tel 0117 929 1740

Further reading

Burns, Brian
Double Bevel Sharpening (booklet)
Available from The Japan Woodworker,
California, USA
Tel: 0015 1052 11810 Fax: 0015 1052 11864

Frid, Tage
*Tage Frid Teaches Woodworking: Book 1
(Joinery, Tools and Techniques)* and
*Tage Frid Teaches Woodworking: Book 2
(Shaping, Veneering, Finishing)* originally
published in separate volumes. Since
reissued in a combined volume entitled
Tage Frid Teaches Woodworking: Books 1 & 2.
Paperback. Taunton Press, USA, 1993
(ISBN 1 56158 068 6)

Hoadley, R. Bruce
Understanding Wood
Hardback. Taunton Press, USA, 1980
(ISBN 0 918804 05 1)

Joyce, Ernest
The Technique of Furniture Making
Hardback. B.T. Batsford, 4th edition,
revised by Alan Peters 1987
(ISBN 0 7134 4407 X)

Krenov, James
The Fine Art of Cabinetmaking
Hardback. Sterling, USA, 1992
(ISBN 0 8069 8572 0)

Landis, Scott
The Workbench Book
Hardback. Taunton Press, USA, 1987
(ISBN 0 918804 76 0)

Odate, Toshio
*Japanese Woodworking Tools: Their Tradition,
Spirit and Use*
Paperback. Stobart Davies, 1998
(ISBN 0 85442 075 4)

Wearing, Robert
*The Essential Woodworker: Skills, Tools
and Methods*
Paperback. B.T. Batsford, 1996
(ISBN 0 7134 8005 X)

Making Woodwork Aids and Devices
Paperback. Revised edition, GMC Publications, 1999
(ISBN 1 86108 129 4)

Handbook of Hardwoods
Hardback. 2nd edition, revised by R. H. Farmer,
H.M.S.O. London, 1988
(ISBN 0 11 470541 0)

This excellent book contains information on reduced
cutting angles as well as much other valuable
information, including movement figures, local
names, bending radii and uses. It is now out of
print, but no serious workshop should be without
it. The Stationery Office in Manchester will print
copies on request. Tel: 0161 834 7201

Metric/Imperial Conversion Chart

mm	inch	mm	inch	mm	inch	mm	inch	mm	inch
1	0.03937	21	0.82677	41	1.61417	160	6.29921	360	14.17322
2	0.07874	22	0.86614	42	1.65354	170	6.69291	370	14.56692
3	0.11811	23	0.90551	43	1.69291	180	7.08661	380	14.96063
4	0.15748	24	0.94488	44	1.73228	190	7.48031	390	15.35433
5	0.19685	25	0.98425	45	1.77165	200	7.87401	400	15.74803
6	0.23622	26	1.02362	46	1.81102	210	8.26771	410	16.14173
7	0.27559	27	1.06299	47	1.85039	220	8.66141	420	16.53543
8	0.31496	28	1.10236	48	1.88976	230	9.05511	430	16.92913
9	0.35433	29	1.14173	49	1.92913	240	9.44881	440	17.32283
10	0.39370	30	1.18110	50	1.96850	250	9.84252	450	17.71653
11	0.43307	31	1.22047	60	2.36220	260	10.23622	460	18.11023
12	0.47244	32	1.25984	70	2.75590	270	10.62992	470	18.50393
13	0.51181	33	1.29921	80	3.14960	280	11.02362	480	18.89763
14	0.55118	34	1.33858	90	3.54330	290	11.41732	490	19.29133
15	0.59055	35	1.37795	100	3.93700	300	11.81102	500	19.68504
16	0.62992	36	1.41732	110	4.33070	310	12.20472		
17	0.66929	37	1.45669	120	4.72440	320	12.59842		
18	0.70866	38	1.49606	130	5.11811	330	12.99212		
19	0.74803	39	1.53543	140	5.51181	340	13.38582		
20	0.78740	40	1.57480	150	5.90551	350	13.77952		

1 mm = .03937 inch
1 cm = .3937 inch
1 m = 3.281 feet
1 inch = 25.4 mm
1 foot = 304.8 mm
1 yard = 914.4 mm

Imperial/Metric Conversion Chart

inch		mm	inch		mm	inch		mm	inch		mm
0	0	0	17/64	0.265625	6.7469	1/2	0.500	12.700	49/64	0.765625	19.4469
1/64	0.015625	0.3969	9/32	0.28125	7.1438	33/64	0.515625	13.0969	25/32	0.78125	19.8438
1/32	0.03125	0.7938	19/64	0.296875	7.5406	17/32	0.53125	13.4938	51/64	0.796875	20.2406
3/64	0.046875	1.1906	5/16	0.3125	7.9375	35/64	0.546875	13.8906	13/16	0.8125	20.6375
1/16	0.0625	1.5875				9/16	0.5625	14.2875			
5/64	0.078125	1.9844	21/64	0.1328125	8.3344	37/64	0.578125	14.6844	53/64	0.828125	21.0344
3/32	0.09375	2.3812	11/32	0.34375	8.7312	19/32	0.59375	15.0812	27/32	0.84375	21.4312
7/64	0.109375	2.7781	23/64	0.359375	9.1281	39/64	0.609375	15.4781	55/64	0.858375	21.8281
1/8	0.125	3.1750	3/8	0.375	9.5250	5/8	0.625	15.8750	7/8	0.875	22.2250
9/64	0.140625	3.5719	25/64	0.390625	9.9219	41/64	0.640625	16.2719	57/64	0.890625	22.6219
5/32	0.15625	3.9688	13/32	0.40625	10.3188	21/32	0.65625	16.6688	29/32	0.90625	23.0188
11/64	0.171875	4.3656	27/64	0.421875	10.7156	43/64	0.671875	17.0656	59/64	0.921875	23.4156
3/16	0.1875	4.7625	7/16	0.4375	11.1125	11/16	0.6875	17.4625	15/16	0.9375	23.8125
13/64	0.203125	5.1594	29/64	0.453125	11.5094	45/64	0.703125	17.8594	61/64	0.953125	24.2094
7/32	0.21875	5.5562	15/32	0.46875	11.9062	23/32	0.71875	18.2562	31/32	0.96875	24.6062
15/64	0.234375	5.9531	31/64	0.484375	12.3031	47/64	0.734375	18.6531	63/64	0.984375	25.0031
1/4	0.250	6.3500				3/4	0.750	19.0500			

1 inch = 1.000 = 25.40 mm

About the author

David Charlesworth runs private courses on the making of fine furniture from his home and workshop at Hartland in north Devon. He trained with Edward Baly, the principal founder member of the Devon Guild of Craftsmen, then turned from making commissioned pieces to teaching.

He regularly contributes articles to *Furniture & Cabinetmaking* magazine, from which this collection was compiled. Details of his courses can be obtained by telephoning David on 01237 441288, via e-mail on davidcharl@aol.com or on the Internet: http://www.davidcharlesworth.co.uk

Index

Index